The Lure of the
mountains

Edited and Selection of Photos by

HERBERT MAEDER

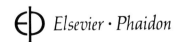 Elsevier · Phaidon

We would like to acknowledge the cooperation of the Swiss Trade Center which furnished photos pages vi-1, 19, 26-27, 89, 101, 114-115, 134.

The photo on pages 80-81 was furnished by the Comet Press of Zurich, Switzerland.

Elsevier • Phaidon

an imprint of PHAIDON PRESS LIMITED

5 Cromwell Place, London SW7 2JL

This edition first published in Great Britain 1975.

Originally published as Lockende Berge © *1971 by Silva-Verlag, Zurich*

Translation copyright © 1975 by Thomas Y. Crowell Company, Inc.

Published in the USA by Thomas Y. Crowell Company, Inc., New York

ISBN 0 7290 0038 9

Designed by Abigail Moseley

PRINTED IN BELGIUM
by OFFSET VAN DEN BOSSCHE

Contents

The Säntis is the highest peak on the Säntis Mountain and the northernmost Alpine peak in Switzerland. It is 2,501 meters above sea level, and the region is constantly covered with snow. World-traveling geologist Albert Heim praised the Säntis Mountain as one of the most beautiful mountains in the world. The Säntis Mountain is a much visited mountain with a lovely view. From a part of the breezy Lisengrat Path which connects the Säntis Mountain with the Altmann (a little lower—2,436 meters), we look southward to the seven Chur Ridges and the higher mountains of St. Gallen and Glarnus.

John Ruskin (1819–1900) The English philosopher, author, and art critic who defended the works of Turner and the new English painting school in his five-volume work on modern painters. This selection is an intelligent and well-founded tribute to the mountains.

1 JOHN RUSKIN

The Mountain Glory

To myself, mountains are the beginning and the end of all natural scenery; in them, and in the forms of inferior landscape that lead to them, my affections are wholly bound up; and though I can look with happy admiration at the lowland flowers, and woods, and open skies, the happiness is tranquil and cold, like that of examining detached flowers in a conservatory, or reading a pleasant book; and if the scenery be resolutely level, insisting upon the declaration of its own flatness in all the detail of it, as in Holland, or Lincolnshire, or Central Lombardy, it appears to me like a prison, and I cannot long endure it. But the slightest rise and fall in the road—a mossy bank at the side of a crag of chalk, with brambles at its brow, overhanging it—a ripple over three or four stones in the stream by the bridge—above all, a wild bit of ferny ground under a fir or two, looking as if, possibly, one might see a hill if one got to the other side of the trees, will instantly give me intense delight, because the shadow, or the hope, of the hills, is in them. . . .

For consider, first, the difference produced in the whole tone of landscape color by the introductions of purple, violet, and deep ultramarine blue, which we owe to mountains. In an ordinary lowland landscape we have the blue of the sky; the green of grass, which I will suppose (and this is an unnecessary concession to the lowlands) entirely fresh and bright; the green of trees; and certain elements of purple, far more rich and beautiful than we generally should think, in their bark and shadows (bare hedges and thickets, or tops of trees, in subdued afternoon sunshine, are nearly perfect purple, and of an exquisite tone), as well as in ploughed fields, and dark ground in general. But among mountains, in *addition* to all this, large unbroken spaces of pure violet and purple are introduced in their distances; and even near, by films of cloud passing over the darkness of ravines or forests, blues are produced of the most subtle tenderness; these azures and purples passing into rose-color of otherwise wholly unattainable delicacy

2

among the upper summits, the blue of the sky being at the same time purer and deeper than in the plains. Nay, in some sense, a person who has never seen the rose-color of the rays of dawn crossing a blue mountain twelve or fifteen miles away, can hardly be said to know what *tenderness* in color means at all; *bright* tenderness he may, indeed, see in the sky or in a flower, but this grave tenderness of the far-away hill-purples he cannot conceive.

Together with this great source of pre-eminence in *mass* of color, we have to estimate the influence of the finished inlaying and enamel-work of the color-jewellery on every stone; and that of the continual variety in species of flower; most of the mountain flowers being, besides, separately lovelier than the lowland ones. . . .

To this supremacy in mosses and flowers we have next to add an inestimable gain in the continual presence and power of water. . . . The mantling of the pools in the rock shadows, with the golden flakes of light sinking down through them like falling leaves, the ringing of the thin currents among the shallows, the flash and the cloud of the cascade, the earthquake and foam-fire of the cataract, the long lines of alternate mirror and mist that lull the imagery of the hills reversed in the blue of morning,—all these things belong to those hills as their undivided inheritance.

To this supremacy in wave and stream is joined a no less manifest pre-eminence in the character of trees. . . . The various action of trees rooting themselves in inhospitable rocks, stooping to look into ravines, hiding from the search of glacier winds, reaching forth to the rays of rare sunshine, crowding down together to drink at sweetest streams, climbing hand in hand among the difficult slopes, opening in sudden dances round the mossy knolls, gathering into companies at rest among the fragrant fields, gliding in grave procession over the heavenward ridges—nothing of this can be conceived among the unvexed and

In the summer, before 5 A.M., the first rays of the morning sun redden the powerful pyramid of the Weisshorn (4,-505 meters). The Bishorn (4,134 meters) is a front peak of the Weisshorn. Of the Valasain 4,000-meter peaks, it is one of the easiest to climb. An imposing military policeman swings along the daring and difficult northern ledge to this peak. The mountain climber moves along this ledge, which continues over the monstrous abyss of the glaciered northeast side and the rocky west wall.

3

unvaried felicities of the lowland forest: while to all these direct sources of greater beauty are added, first the power of redundance,—the mere quantity of foliage visible in the folds and on the promontories of a single Alp being greater than that of an entire lowland landscape (unless a view from some cathedral tower); and to this charm of redundance, that of clearer *visibility*,—tree after tree being constantly shown in successive height, one behind another, instead of the mere tops and flanks of masses, as in the plains; and the forms of multitudes of them continually defined against the clear sky, near and above, or against white clouds entangled among their branches, instead of being confused in dimness of distance.

Finally, to this supremacy in foliage we have to add the still less questionable supremacy in clouds. . . . There are effects by tens of thousands, forever invisible and inconceivable to the inhabitant of the plains, manifested among the hills in the course of one day. The mere power of familiarity with the clouds, of walking with them and above them, alters and renders clear our whole conception of the baseless architecture of the sky; and for the beauty of it, there is more in a single wreath of early cloud, pacing its way up an avenue of pines, or pausing among the points of their fringes, than in all the white heaps that fill the arched sky of the plains from one horizon to the other. And of the nobler cloud manifestations,—the breaking of their troublous seas against the crags, their black spray sparkling with lightning; or the going forth of the morning along their pavements of moving marble, level-laid between dome and dome of snow;—of these things there can be as little imagination or understanding in an inhabitant of the plains as of the scenery of another planet than his own.

And, observe, all these superiorities are matters plainly measurable and calculable, not in any wise to be referred to estimate of *sensation*. Of the grandeur or expression of the hills I have not spoken; how far they are great, or strong, or terrible, I do not for the moment consider, because vastness, and strength, and terror, are not to all minds subjects of desired contemplation. It may make no difference to some men whether a natural object be large or small, whether it be strong or feeble. But loveliness of color, perfectness of form, endlessness of change, wonderfulness of structure, are precious to all undiseased human minds; and the superiority of the mountains in all these things to the lowland is, I repeat, as measurable as the richness of a painted window matched with a white one, or the wealth of a museum compared with that of a simply furnished chamber. They seem to have been built for the human race, as at once their schools and cathedrals; full of treasures of illuminated manuscript for the scholar, kindly in simple lessons to the worker, quiet in pale cloisters for the thinker, glorious in holiness for the worshipper.

Herbert Maeder (1930–) The photographer-journalist Herbert Maeder, who grew up in the small town of Wil in eastern Switzerland, is an enthusiastic mountain climber. In books, magazines and newspapers he likes to report on adventures in alpinism.

2 HERBERT MAEDER
Discovering the Swiss Mountains

"The Alps are the pride of any Swiss who has made his home at the foot of the mountains. Their existence has an indescribably farreaching influence on his entire life.

In part, his personal, spiritual, social and political life depends on them. He loves them almost instinctively; after he has left them he longs with every fiber of his heart to be back. His love for the mountains is perhaps even greater than his love of nature." (Friedrich von Tschudi, 1853, from *Animals in the Alpine Regions.*)

Friedrich von Tschudi, the scholar and statesman, wrote these words during the tumultuous times of the Age of Enlightenment. The new federal state had just been founded, and the Swiss experienced a new feeling for their homeland. Do his words still have value today, do they still touch us? I think so. During Tschudi's time the discovery and the conquest of the Alps was in full swing. It had become fashionable to travel in the Alps, and above all science became interested in the nature of the mountains.

Two spiritual movements had awakened the love and the enthusiasm for the mountains: the Renaissance and the Enlightenment. Up to the beginning of the Renaissance, the Alps were more feared than loved. At that time fantasy portrayed the almost inaccessible mountain regions as being inhabited by dragons and other monsters. Fear, and not reverence, dominated the common attitude towards the mountains. Our Alps were not thrones of Gods like fiery Mount Aetna, or Fugiyama, or the peaks of the Himalayas.

We do not know what the original alpine population felt in regard to the mountains. There are no written documents about the peasants and shepherds who in medieval times went over the glaciers of the mountain passes—like Col d'Herens (3,462 meters) or Col Collon (3,117 meters), for instance—with their cattle.

It can be assumed that the mountain people knew their way around the

5

mountains, but they probably did not climb higher than necessary for driving to pasture, hunting and trading.

During antiquity and in medieval times the Alps formed a stubborn obstacle to trading and to military expeditions. When in 154 B.C. the Romans started on their first wars of conquest through the mountains, only three narrow paths were known as Alpine crossings: probably the Great St. Bernard, the Mont-Cenis and the Brenner Passes. The great colonizers of antiquity built the first roads across the Alps. Today we can still walk in their tracks and can admire their foundations and bridges. Roman coins found on the Theodul saddle give evidence that even glacier passes were used in those days. The highest road built by the Romans led over the Great St. Bernard (2,472 meters). Since in such altitudes there is snow for nine months, using this pass was often a struggle against storm, snow and cold. In 962 Bernard von Menthon founded on the pass the famous Sankt-Bernard-Cloister, for many centuries the highest winter domicile in Switzerland. The monks were obliged to give shelter to all travelers, regardless of position or creed, and to help people in emergency. They were helped in their task by big, strong dogs which are still known today as St. Bernards. Similar hostels sprang up on various passes. Traffic on these few alpine passes did not even stop during winter. Everyone who is used to mountains can easily imagine what it was like to cross a 2,500-meter-high pass on foot in the middle of winter. Besides unrealistic superstition the fear of the mountains is based on very realistic conditions.

In 1444, at the beginning of the great spiritual movement which we call the Renaissance, Konrad Witz painted his famous altar picture, "St. Peter Fishing". In the background of the seascape is a glacial mountain range—the Montblanc massif. The painter took the liberty of painting this biblical scene in the setting of Lake Geneva, which was familiar to him. His style of painting the mountains in this work of art is unique: they are not stylized, as they had been up to that time, but truly real mountains. Many artists of that time were searching for nature, above all the gifted Leonardo da Vinci (1452–1519), whose sketches of mountains do not show fantastic scenery populated by dragons, but rather scenery with exact topographical features. As usual, the artists were ahead of their time, but the scientists did not follow too much later.

In 1518 Joachim von Watt of St. Gallen, a doctor and learned humanist and later reformer, mayor and governor, went to Lucerne with three companions in order to climb the Pilatus. There was a legend that the body of the governor of Judea was resting in the little mountain lake near the Pilatus, and any disturbance by human beings would have terrible consequences. The authorities had therefore prohibited anyone from climbing the Pilatus. When in 1307 six young clergymen tried to conquer the mountain, they went to jail for it. Vadian climbed the Pilatus and nothing happened. In his description Vadian called the Pilatus legend "nonsense".

6

Clouds are forming above one of the gendarmes of the Weisshorn. The air is saturated with humidity; a thunderstorm is brewing. Two mountain climbers are on the descent. They will reach the protection of the Weisshorn Hut in time. The eastern ridge offers the easiest and safest ascent to the Weisshorn. It is known as the normal route and it was also used by John Tyndall, J. J. Bennen, and Ulrich Wenger, who on August 19, 1861 were the first to climb the peak.

Vadian's excursion to the Pilatus was very reasonable: he wanted to disprove the superstition. How far this ambition was supported by his interest and love of nature is uncertain.

In 1555 Zurich scientist Konrad Gessner, one of the great humanists, repeated the excursion to the Pilatus, this time with approval by the authorities. Gessner not only confirmed the absurdity of the Pilatus legend, but he was also very enthusiastic about the beauty of the mountains and the fascination of mountain climbing. "All our senses are stimulated in the mountains. The whole body is refreshed by the cool air which covers the entire surface of the body and of which the lungs take full breaths. As Homer said, 'The breeze of the cold Borea refreshes us'. On the other hand, after having endured wind and cold, one can warm up in the sunshine or at a fire in the shepherd's hut. And the eyes enjoy gazing at the beautiful mountains, rocks, forests, valleys, brooks and meadows, because everything is so very colorful. As far as the shape of all the objects that the eye beholds is concerned—the rocks, ravines and gorges—they are so wonderful and strange and so admirable for their greatness and altitude."

Konrad Gessner is rightfully called the forefather of alpinism. Even in 1541 he pledged in a letter to Jakob Vogel: "I made up my mind, my learned friend, from now on and as long as God gives me life, to climb at least one mountain or more each year at a time when the flowers are blooming, partly in order to get to know them and partly in order to exercise the body and to delight the mind." He then goes on to praise enthusiastically the joys of the mountains: "It is such a pleasure for the mind to admire the immense masses of the mountains, like a spectacle and to lift up the head almost into the clouds." The scientist can only look down upon those who do not show any appreciation for the mountains. "I therefore maintain that he who does not find the mountains worthy of his admiration is an enemy of nature."

These humanists were straightforward people. They did not believe in indecision but instead went ahead in their search for the understanding of nature. We find a similar enthusiasm for the mountains only with the Bern humanist Aretius, whose real name was Benedikt Marti. In 1557 Aretius had climbed

Between Lake Sämti and Lake Fählen near the Säntis is a huge limestone rock whose rough stone is ideal for children in their first attempts to climb. Climbing rocks is a natural activity, attractive to both boys and girls.

Niesen and Stockhorn and had done some botanical research. However, his interest in science was not his only reason: "Who would not admire and love the Alps, visit them with pleasure, hike and climb them? I can only call them stupid simpletons, imbecile blockheads, lazy turtles who are not touched by such beauty. I cannot express the longing and love I feel for the mountains and there is no other place where I would rather be."

When we read such enthusiastic words today we always have to keep in mind that in those days it was difficult to travel in the mountains and that by no means were they visited and appreciated by a large segment of the population. The humanistic scientists of that time were a rare exception and only the pioneers of a movement which a hundred years later became more widespread.

In 1574 theologian and humanist Josias Simler (1530–1576), who was a friend of Konrad Gessner's, published in Zurich the first book about the Alps in Latin, *De Alpibus Commentarius*. In this encyclopedia Simler summarized the entire knowledge of his time. Unfortunately, Simler, who suffered from gout, was unable to climb mountains, and therefore his book lacks Gessner's ardour and enthusiasm and the exactness of personal observation. However, some chapters are very interesting for the understanding of early alpinism.

In chapter XIV, "Difficulties and Dangers of Travelling in the Alps and How to Overcome Them", are found valuable details about the equipment of the mountain traveler in those days: "The difficult conditions of the mountain paths are often augmented by precipices and steep slopes, especially when the roads are icy. Travelers, shepherds and hunters who are used to roaming through the mountains have various remedies. In order to walk on icy, slippery terrain, they would wear iron soles with three spikes not unlike horseshoes. . . . In other areas canes with iron tips are used when climbing steep slopes or in deep snow. Sometimes shepherds and hunters would cut branches from trees, mostly pine

On Lake Gräppelen near Obertoggenburg. Held by father's or mother's hand the small child gets to know the beauty of the foothills of the Alps. Perhaps the timid steps across the rickety bridge are the beginning of a mountain-climbing career.

9

trees, and would sit on them and slide down steep slopes while riding on them."

Simler also reports about crossing glacier passes. Undoubtedly this is the first literary document concerning the crossing of a glacier, and the first time when mountain guides are mentioned. "Furthermore the old ice across which one often has to walk has deep crevices, three to four feet wide and often more; he who falls into them no doubt will perish. It often happens that such crevices are covered by the freshly fallen or windswept snow; therefore the travelers who cross the Alps would hire guides who knew these dangerous places. They use a rope to which they tie some of the travelers following them. The guide goes first, inspects the path with a long stick and looks for crevices covered by snow. If he unexpectedly falls into one of them, his companions, who are tied to him, hold him and pull him out."

The greatest alpine danger in those days, just like today, is present during winter's white splendor. Josias Simler had some very strange and some amazingly realistic notions of the character and size of avalanches. He probably had some original reports: ". . . they tumble down with a noise that seems to make the earth tremble, and if one does not know what is happening, it sounds like distant thunder. However, these avalanches do not go down everywhere and during the whole year, but only on steep slopes without trees. They occur mostly at the time in spring when the snow melts and gets soft or when, in the fall or winter, large masses of freshly fallen snow start sliding down icy, steep hills. There are two kinds of avalanches: one, when freshly fallen snow forms into balls and slides down a slope; and the other, formed by old snow which takes part of the topsoil with it. The latter ones are bigger and do more damage. Several years ago there was a huge avalanche in the Rhine valley in Rhätien, near the Rhine source, which devastated a forest of tall pine trees and took the trunks with it. Sixty or more Swiss soldiers who were marching through the Alps were buried under masses of snow. Sometimes, however, people who are caught by an avalanche stay alive under the snow, are found and are brought back from the depths."

The humanists mentioned before are considered the actual pioneers of alpinism. They either climbed themselves or increased the fund of knowledge about the mountains. One name should not be left out, even if it is only indirectly linked with alpinism: Theophrastus von Hohenheim, called Paracelsus (1493–1541). This forerunner of modern medicine was a well-travelled man who crossed a number of mountain passes. He was not only familiar with the nature of the mountains, but also he himself felt that he was a son of the mountains. His mother was from Einsiedeln. "I am from Einsiedeln, my country is Switzerland," he said of himself. The professors in Basle, where he lectured for some time, were very much annoyed that he held his lectures in German and not in Latin. They teased him and called him "Donkey of Einsiedeln". He did not mind but rather teased his noble colleagues that they would not "even deserve to carry the

10

Visibility in the mountains is never better than on beautiful fall days. Behind the steep, elegant profile of the western edge of the Altmann, the Rhine valley, covered with haze, stretches south towards Graubünden. Above that the jagged range of the Bündner Mountains forms the horizon, crowned by its highest peak, the Piz Bernina, 4,049 meters, which at the same time is the last and most eastern 4,000-meter mountain of the Alps.

The landscape coins and influences the facial expression and the soul of man. Bonifaz Kühne from Vasön is a shepherd on Tersol, the highest pasture of the St. Gallen highlands. His hut is at an altitude of 2,000 meters and can only be reached on a steep, difficult path. In the summer of 1970 Bonifaz Kühne spent his eightieth year on Tersol. With his long shepherd's crook the eighty-five year old mastered the path on foot, as he had always done.

urinal for Hippocrates." He excused his rough manners with the fact that he was a child of the mountains. "By nature I am not a very refined person, and my countrymen are not. We were not raised on a diet of figs, mead nor wheat bread, but on cheese, milk and oat bread: this cannot produce very refined fellows." He was the first to explore and publicize the alpine thermal and mineral springs. He and the other humanists have done a great deal for the exploration of the mountains.

Only during the sixteenth century were the Alps truly discovered and explored. The reports, letters and appeals of the humanists were like a flourish of trumpets. Were they heard? Only by a few. The great prophets of the mountains died and took their love of nature with them into their graves.

In the history of mountain climbing the seventeenth century is a desolate chapter. There were setbacks in the entire cultural life. Wars destroyed half of Europe and paralyzed man's quest for knowledge. There was the Thirty Year's War, the plague and general misery. What was known of the Alps seemed to be lost. In his description of Switzerland (1627) David l'Hermite stated that the people of the Alps would bury their dead in ice because they did not have enough soil, and that they were so stingy that they drove their cattle into the highest mountain where, in complete solitude, they forgot to speak their language, just like animals. Man of the seventeenth century was too busy in his struggle for survival to have time to be interested in the mountains.

After an interval of one century it was again the natural scientists who went out to explore the mountains. During the years 1702–11 Zurich doctor Johann Jakob Scheuchzer, a scholar with a preference for geology and physics, roamed through the Swiss mountains with his students. Gessner's enthusiasm for the mountains comes alive once more in Scheuchzer's work *Itinera per Helvetiae alpinas regiones.* "If you want to achieve something in your studies of this subject

12

you cannot sit at home by the fire and indulge in melancholy thoughts, but you have to go out and hike through mountains and valleys. . . . In these wild and lonely regions I found more enjoyment than at the feet of the great Aristotle, Epicurus and Cartesius. . . .

In 1729 a signal was sent from Bern into the cultural world which could not be missed and which had great significance for the general attitude towards the mountains. The signal was a poem with the title "The Alps"; the author was Albrecht von Haller (1708–1777), physician and natural scientist. Young Haller had made a poem of his impressions on a trip through the mountains. Haller did not praise any adventures in the high mountains but rather extolled the happy life of the shepherds and peasants, which he compared to the corruption in the cities and at the courts of royalty.

The time was ripe for such thoughts and feelings. Haller's "The Alps" became a great literary success; the author lived to see eleven editions and several translations of it. It was an expression of a new feeling towards nature, and it drew the attention of the educated world to the scenic beauty of Switzerland. The pomposity of the poem sounds strange to us today. As a sample, here is the last verse:

> Blessed is he who with self-raised oxen can plough the soil of his own fields; who is clothed in pure wool, adorned with wreaths of leaves, and enjoys an unseasoned meal made of sweet milk; who can sleep carefree on soft grass, refreshed by Zephyr's breeze and cool waterfalls; who has never been awakened on high seas by rough waves, nor by the sound of trumpets at troubled times; who is satisfied with his lot and never wants to improve it! Luck is much too poor to increase his well-being.

Haflinger horses on their way to the Suretta pasture. During the last few years the tough, stocky mountain horse with the blond mane and tail has become very popular in the Alps. In the area of the Suretta Lakes above Splügen every summer about fifty Haflingers roam about the vast pasture.

The Berner Haller anticipated in his poetic thoughts and feelings were formulated more precisely and effectively later on by Jean-Jacques Rousseau of Geneva: The "natural freedom" of man, the democratic republic as the ideal state and "back to nature" as mankind's goal. Rousseau's works awakened man and challenged him to act. In his novel *The New Heloise* (1761) primitive, natural feelings were victorious over the unnatural way of life in the drawing-rooms, and

in his *Social Contract* (1762) the cruelty of absolutism was confronted with a true government of the people. Rousseau showed the way back to nature and forward towards revolution.

Rousseau's numerous disciples wanted to see the soil on which such a new spirit grew; and they wanted to get to know the scenery which Rousseau describes in his *Confessions:* "They know what I mean by beautiful scenery. I need brooks, rocks, pine trees, dark forests, rough winding paths and abysses."

This refreshing climate of the Enlightenment gave a new impulse to the research of the Alps. In 1787 physicist and geologist Horace-Bénédict de Saussure (1740–1799) climbed the highest peak of the Alps, Montblanc, with a large expedition. A year before, on August 8, 1786, Jacques Balmat and physician Michel Gabriel Paccard had climbed the peak for the first time. Saussure was a very ambitious scientist. On Montblanc, and while climbing many other mountains, he made scientific experiments. Saussure's four-volume *Voyage dans les Alpes* gives testimony to his untiring research.

The need to describe and present the Alps was awakened. Johann Rudolf Meyer (1739–1813), a manufacturer from Aarau, asked engineer and topographer Johann Heinrich Weiss of Strassburg and model-maker Joachim Eugen Müller of Engelberg to make a relief map of Switzerland on a scale of 1:60,000. Based on this highly praised model, the first atlas of Switzerland was engraved in copper during the years 1796–1802. On sixteen pages on a scale of 1:120,000 a vertical perspective is used which, for the first time, gives an undistorted picture of the topographical features.

During 1811 and 1812 Meyer's sons, Johann Rudolf the younger and Hieronymus, took long hikes between the Grimsel-Pass and Lötschenlücke with the purpose of improving the maps made by their father. At this time they conquered one of the most beckoning peaks of the Alps, the Jungfrau, on August 3, 1811.

Franz Joseph Hugi, a glacier expert and geologist from Solothurn, tried on August 19, 1828 to reach the highest peak of the Berner Highlands, the Finsteraarhorn. His guides, Jakob Leuthold and Johann Wahren, reached the peak

In the beginning of July cattle climb over the snow of an avalanche up to the Tersol pasture. This sunny pasture on the south side of the Pizol can only be reached across steep slopes where avalanches come down in winter and spring. Pasture time on Tersol is short—only eight to ten weeks.

while Hugi had to stay back because of a foot injury. Today the ridge under the peak bears Hugi's name.

With the exception of Meyer's cartographers, there were not many people in the mountains at the turn of the century. The ideals of Rousseau and other humanists had logically led to the French Revolution in 1789, and the effects were soon to be felt in the alpine state of Switzerland. War and turmoil again brought a stop to interest in the mountains.

Only in Bündnerland was there an indefatigable alpinist—Placidus a Spescha (1752–1833). This highly intelligent and gifted monk was a pioneer and an outsider. He called himself a geographer, but he was a man of universal interests who occupied himself with botany, mineralogy, geology, history, economics and

Winter sunrise on Rigi-Kulm (1,797 meters). Fog covers the valleys. Above the Rossberg in the foreground one can see the mountains of eastern Switzerland in the distance. With the construction of the Rigi railroads from Vitznau and from Arth in 1871 and 1874, the Alps began to be opened to mass tourism. But tourists of the last century still took their time when admiring a sunrise.

15

various other subjects. He had a mineralogical collection of great significance and in 1800 wrote a book titled *Instructions on Taking Mountain Excursions,* a regular textbook for mountain climbers.

Pater Placidus a Spescha could write from his own rich experience because he had succeeded in climbing several mountains. He was the first to climb, among others, the Rheinwaldhorn, the Oberalpstock, Piz Aul, Piz Terri; and he almost succeeded in climbing the Tödi.

Placidus a Spescha had the same fiery spirit as Rousseau—he was an intrepid fighter with an independent judgment. However, it was not only his thirst for knowledge which made him go to the mountains. When he was seventy he confessed: "My body became heavy and my mind became sad because of too much sitting and thinking. Then I started moving, sweating out the evil and superfluous fluids. I came home purified and as light as a bird.

"During my travels, I observed all the objects I came in contact with—the birds and how they fly, and deer grazing and jumping, the plants growing and blooming, the glaziers cracking, and how stones and rocks, ice and snow tear loose and tumble downhill. I enjoy this crashing and thundering, as well as the growing life, more than any pomp or music in this world."

This new appreciation of nature, beautifully expressed by Spescha's words, showed its effects in many ways. In eighteenth-century painted landscapes the mountains had always looked like artificial backdrops. This was changed by Alexandre Calame (1810–1864) from western Switzerland. Calame's alpine landscapes showed the greatness and power of the mountains and gave testimony to his own experience.

A picture like "Monte Rosa Chain during Sunrise" presents the high mountains as they are still seen today by mountain climbers. As early as 1830 the English painter William Turner (1775–1851) painted Monte Rosa during storm and rain. Turner loved strange light effects, fog, and night scenes. He was a precursor of the Impressionists and his landscapes became very popular. Turner gave fresh impetus to the natural sciences and the romantic feeling for nature—the bases for the discovery of the Alps, which was not making good progress at the time.

For many years Louis Agassiz (1807–1873) and Edouard Desor (1811–1882) of Neuenburg explored the glaciers of the Berner Highlands. Under a boulder on the central moraine of the Unteraar glacier they had a primitive shelter, their "Hôtel des Neuchâtelois". Their *Etudes sur les glaciers,* published in 1840, was a basic work on glaciers. In 1842, in the course of his research, Desor climbed the Great Lauteraarhorn, and two years later the Rosenhorn. In 1845 Agassiz reached the Haslejungfrau. Agassiz continued his studies of glaciers later on in the United States, where he was Professor of Geology and Zoology at Harvard.

Important pioneers in the exploration of the Alps, among others, were the geologists Arnold Escher von der Linth (1807–1872) (the son of Hans Konrad Escher von der Linth, who suggested and planned the Linth correction), Professor Bernhard Studer (1794–1887) in Bern, Gottlieb Ludwig Theobald (1810–1869) in Chur, and Rudolf Theodor Simler (1833–1873) in Bern. Karl Ludwig Rütimeyer (1825–1895) of the University of Basle was world-famous as a broadminded and perspicacious zoologist.

Friedirch von Tschudi (1820–1886), minister, scholar, author and politician, published in 1853 *Animals of the Alpine World*, a book which was translated into many languages and was reprinted again and again.

During the years 1832–1864, under the direction of General Henri Dufour, the "Topographic Map of Switzerland" was created, a cartographical masterpiece of 25 pages scaled at 1:100,000. One of Dufour's most enterprising topographers was Johann Wilhelm Fortunat Coaz (1822–1918) from Bünden. While surveying, Coaz climbed a number of peaks—in 1845 the Hoch-Ducan and the Flüela-Weisshorn, and in 1850 the highest peak in Bünden, the 4,049-meter-high Piz Bernina. Later on Coaz became chief forester for Bünden and then for the Swiss Confederation. In this capacity he strongly advocated afforestation and the blockage of avalanches. Today a SAC shelter in the Bernina area bears his name.

As we have seen, an interest in mountain climbing can be traced back to the humanists; and we have found Rousseau's feeling for nature to be the basis for a new enthusiasm for the mountains. A number of peaks were climbed. Trips into the Alps were fashionable.

But was there already an alpinism? Hardly. Almost always there was a reason for the excursions into the mountains. The geologists hammered away at the rocks, the botanists collected plants, the topographers surveyed the territory,

View of the Val della Porta, a side valley of Verzascatals in the Tessim. Even during the high season of tourism the Tessim Mountains are very isolated. Many mountain pastures are abandoned and only gorse grows today where fifty years ago cows were grazing.

17

the zoologists observed the behavior of the wild animals. Mountain climbing just for the sake of mountain climbing—an enjoyment, a sport? No!

Even the early Swiss mountain climbers who were not scientists and liked to call themselves "montanists" felt more like explorers than athletes. Sport, and, in connection with it, alpinism, came with the Englishmen.

Because of intensive industrialization and world-wide colonialism, a rich middle class had developed in Victorian England. Besides the first industrial proletariat—in 1845 Engels published his revolutionary book, *The Situation of the Working Class in England*—there were men with money, time and an adventurous spirit. A few of them were natural scientists like John Tyndall (1820–1893), the glacier expert, and John Ball (1818–1889), the botanist. Most of them were lawyers, ministers, financiers, high officials, businessmen. These men literally threw themselves into the Alps and started mountain climbing as a purely athletic activity. Alpinism was born. As early as 1857 they founded the exclusive Alpine Club. Only persons of high social standing who were tested mountain climbers were allowed to join. John Ball was elected as the first president. He was a man of great alpine experience who soon published the first *Guide for the Western Alps*. The aim of the Alpine Club was not to make mountain climbing more popular. They never thought of building shelters. Their purpose was social exclusivity, an exchange of experience and athletic achievement. In 1854 the English conquered the Wetterhorn, and up to 1865, the climbing of the Matterhorn, there was an incredible number of conquered mountains. In a single decade alone the English undertook more than sixty first climbings. These years are known in history as the "Golden Age of Alpinism".

However, the English did not do it all by themselves; native mountain guides took part in almost all of their undertakings. The people of the mountains contributed their share in the conquest of the high Alps. Names like Christian Almer (1826–1897) and Melchior Anderegg (1827–1914) were already a legend during their lifetimes. Very often the experience and strong muscles of the mountain guides were the cause of their masters' success.

Following are some of the first climbings during the "Golden Age". Incidentally, in those days there were no shelters. The men either climbed up directly from the valley or camped out on the mountain. In 1855 Messrs. G. and S. Smith, Hudson, Birbeck and Stevenson, together with guide Ulrich Lauener from Lauterbrunn, reached the highest peak of the Monte Rosa—the Dufour Peak. In 1857 S. Porges, together with Christian Almer and U. and Ch. Kaufmann conquered the Monk. In the same year E. Anderson, with Christian Almer and Peter Bohren, climbed the Little Schreckhorn. In 1858 there was another brilliant achievement by Christian Almer. He guided, with Peter Bohren, Chr. Barrington up the uninviting Eiger. The Dom, the highest mountain which is located entirely in Switzerland, was climbed the same year by J. L. Davies and guide J. zum Taugwald. Since there was no inn, the party had spent the night

18

From the Titlis (3,239 meters) one can look over the Small Titlis and see the Wetterhorn group in the distance. The Titlis, formerly called Wendenstock or Nollen, is supposed to have been climbed in 1739 by a monk from Engelberg. Since the construction of a cable car, skiers can ride up to its peak even in summer and enjoy the scenic view.

with the vicar of Randa, had left at one o'clock in the morning, climbed the 4,545 meter mountain via the Festi-Saddle, and reached Zermatt in the evening just in time for the Table d'hôte.

In 1859 F. F. Tuckett, with guides J. J. Bennen and P. Bohren, reached the second highest peak of the Berner Highlands, the Aletschhorn. In the same year Sir Leslie Stephen planned to conquer the wild rocky pyramid of the Bietschhorn. He succeeded in climbing it and in his book, *The Playground of Europe,* he tells, in a very humorous way, about this bold adventure.

In 1860 the indefatigable Stephen, together with the king of the guides, Melchior Anderegg, succeeded in climbing the icy Blümlisalphorn and the broad back of the Alphubel. A year later, with Christian and Peter Michel and Christian Kaufmann, he ascended the Great Schreckhorn, one of those famous colossal rock formations which for a long time was said to be unconquerable. In his description of this adventure, he flirted with the glory of the first climber: "It is very likely that the Schreckhorn will outlast the British Constitution as well as the thirty-nine Christian dogmas. As long as it exists and as long as Murray and Baedeker will tell future generations about its wonders and beauties, the fame of the conqueror who once clung to the hem of its snowy garment will survive."

In spite of his success, Stephen was a very reasonable man. He once wrote: "I detest the widespread opinion that people hiking in the Alps are the heroes of an adventure in the mountains. In order to tell the truth, I have to admit when reporting about my ascents that it was Michel, Anderegg or Lauener who made it possible with their skill, strength and courage; and for them it was even more difficult because they had to carry a heavy knapsack and, on top of that, they had to worry about a tourist."

In 1861 glacier expert John Tyndall, Director of the Royal Institute in London, together with Johann Joseph Bennen from Laax, climbed the Weisshorn, one of the highest and most beautiful peaks of the Alps.

J. L. Davies, who was the first to climb the Dom, mastered four years later, in 1862, the difficult peak next to it—the Täschhorn. His guides were J. and S. T. Taugwalder and J. Summermatter.

A cold winter morning in the middle of summer. On the Balmeregghorn (2,255 meters) above the Melchsee pasture the temperature has dropped to minus twelve degrees centigrade in July. A few days before, hikers had walked across mountain pastures in bloom. Such changes in the weather are not infrequent in the Alps and often greatly endanger man and animal. In the background, the Titlis massif.

The evening sun makes one of the limestone ridges of the Diablerets-Stocks (3,209 meters) shine. In the center of the picture is the Argentine, a jagged, rocky ridge with plate-like walls which is ideal for climbing. In the background, the Dents du Midi (3,257 meters), that high mountain ridge which lends the alpine character to the scenery of Lake Geneva.

In the same summer, Thomas Stuart Kennedy, with J. B. Croz and J. Kronig, succeeded in conquering the unfriendly Dent Blanche. Melchior Anderegg, the great guide from Zaun, near Meiringen, was more than just a local guide. He followed his adventurous masters wherever they went. In 1863 he and P. Perren guided R. S. McDonald and F. C. Grove up the Dent d'Herens and the Monte Rosa (Parrot Peak). Even though the English concentrated their main activities on the Wallis District and the Berner Highlands, with their numerous mountains of 4,000 meters and higher, they were also interested in other areas. In 1862 Melchior Anderegg guided L. Stephen and T. S. Kennedy up the Monte della Disgrazia, which stands all by itself; and in 1863 E. W. Buxton, with three guides

This limestone formation in the Säntis district looks like frozen waves. Entire mountain massifs are built from such deposits. The different water solubility accounts for the often bizarre shapes of the rocks.

Granite boulders covered with lichen at the foot of the Badile in the Bergell district. The lichens climb up to the highest peaks and their colors and shapes delight the eye of the mountaineers. However, wet lichens are dangerous for the climber because they make the rocks very slippery.

and four companions, climbed the Piz Palü, one of the most beautifully shaped icy giants of the Alps.

L. Stephen, R. S. MacDonald and T. C. Grove mastered, in 1864, with M. and J. Anderegg and J. Bischoff, the Jungfrau of the Rot Valley. This ascent had a special significance. For it was the first time a peak which had already been climbed was mastered via a different and far more difficult route. This started the "route alpinism". The goal did not matter as much any more as the route by which it was reached. The same party, but without MacDonald, climbed the difficult Zinalrothorn via the north Ridge during that summer.

With the climbing of the Matterhorn in 1865, the "Golden Age" reached its zenith and its end. The most monumental obelisk of the Alps was often described as being unclimbable. This made the elite of the mountaineers feel even more attracted to the isolated peak. Edward Whymper, a twenty-five-year-old illustrator, had made several attempts from the Italian side of the mountain but was unsuccessful. On July 13 he climbed with a party of seven men to a shelter at the Hörnli Ridge. He had teamed up with Reverend Charles Hudson, an alpinist of the highest caliber. With him were also Lord Francis Douglas, Robert D. Hadow, the guides Michel Croz (Chamonix) and the Taugwalders, father and son.

They were successful. The roped party which started the same day towards the peak from the Italian side had to turn back. The most famous peak of the Alps had been climbed, the unattainable achieved. However, the descent ended in a catastrophe. Whymper returned to Zermatt with only the two Taugwalders. The bodies of the other members of the roped party, after having plunged down the north wall, remained, with every bone broken, on the glacier of the Matterhorn. The Matterhorn tragedy found a world-wide echo and put a damper on the joyous game of alpinism.

22

When we look at the chronicle of the "Golden Age" today, we have to admit it—the English did it! In the race for the highest peaks of our Alps the Swiss mountaineers only played a minor role—the English were victorious. What did the Swiss mountaineers do during that time? Were there no Swiss alpinists? Did the Swiss remain "montanists" who liked to roam around the mountains for scientific reasons and did not care for mountain climbing as a sport?

The Swiss mountaineers were not inactive. Their contributions to the discovery of the mountain peaks were greater than it seems. Bern patrician and mountain engineer Edmund von Fellenberg (1838–1902) was the most important discoverer of the Berner Alps. Between Wellhorn and Wildstrubel he climbed every important peak, some for the first, many for the second or third time. Some of the men of the Alpine Club were his friends, but also his athletic rivals. After H. H. George, an Englishman, was the first to make the spectacular northern ascent on the Jungfrau, Fellenberg took revenge and in 1866 was the first to climb the Monk via the steep northwest bulwark.

He carried out this glacial ascent, which is still highly respected and difficult today, with guides Peter Egger and Christian Michel. Edmund von Fellenberg's list of tours boasts proud names: Wildstrubel, Little and Big Doldenhorn, Weisse Frau, Silberhorn, Lauterbrunner Breithorn, and Wellhorn were first climbed by him. He was the first to conquer the dreaded Schreckhorn from the southeast and the Bietschhorn via the western ridge.

Also, Berner governor and notary Gottlieb Studer (1804–1890) could account for twenty-two first climbings, among others the Wildhorn, the Big Wannenhorn and the Studerhorn. Very noteworthy are Studer's drawings of panoramas and his chronicles of alpinism. His book, *About Ice and Snow,* contains the history of the discovery of the Swiss mountains and has become a standard reference in the literature on the mountains. Businessman J. J. Weilenmann from St. Gallen, after several years of business travel in North and South America, devoted himself with enthusiasm to mountain climbing. After twenty years he could adorn his cane by burning 350 names of mountains and passes into it with a burning glass, among them a large number of first climbings such as the Monte Leone (1859), the Fluchthorn (1861) with F. Pöll, the Mont Blanc de Cheilon (1865) with J. Felly, the Piz Buin with J. A. Specht and two guides. Under the title *The Snow-Covered Mountains,* J. J. Weilenmann very vividly describes his mountain feats. Many trips he undertook alone. In his report about the climbing of the Fluchthorn he complains, "The tourist really plays a very subordinate role if he has efficient guides who think, look out and reconnoiter for him, who draw his attention to safe and unsafe steps, help him up or down, and scold him when he does not strictly follow their orders—in short, they guide him like a machine which has no will or power of judgment of its own."

While the members of the Alpine Club were in the midst of conquering the

Two boys have climbed the steps of the south wall of the Scherenturm. In accordance with a world-wide custom of mountain climbers, they shake hands. In the background is the Scherenspitz (Scissor Tip), a peak which from this side looks indeed like the tip of a slightly open scissor. This attractive climbing territory with easy routes for the beginner lies in the western part of the Säntis massif.

highest peaks of the Alps, there was a meeting on April 19, 1863 of a small number of Swiss mountain climbers at the station restaurant of Olten in order to found the Swiss Alpenclub. Berner geologist and chemist Dr. Rudolf Theodor Simler (1833–1873) had suggested the founding of this club of which he was elected president. His secretary was the very daring Edmund von Fellenberg. During the first year the Club had 257 members in eight sections. The goals of the Swiss Alpenclub (SAC) were: exploring the Alps, disseminating alpine publications and facilitating mountain climbing by providing more suitable shelters in the mountains. Already in the first year a primitive club shelter was constructed on the Grünhorn (Tödi). The glacial areas of the Tödi and of the Clariden were

24

declared by the Club to be the first to be explored. In the chronicle of the first yearbook, we learn of the high repute which was immediately enjoyed by the Alpenclub. It tells about the Bern Section, which under the presidency of the highly esteemed Governor Studer acquired sixty-six members by the end of the year, among them a large number of scientists, montanists and artists. Besides this, it also had the honor of having the heads of the Swiss Confederation, i. e., the President and the Chancellor, join its ranks and later on another member of the Federal Council. It was indeed a distinguished club which even in the first year had three members of the Federal Government belonging to it.

This fact also proved how important society considered mountain climbing. The yearbooks which followed are an enormously rich documentation of the exploration of the Alps. The goals of the SAC were quite different from those of the Alpine Club. The latter was a club of the elite with very ambitious athletic aims, while the SAC had broader goals. Through the construction and mainte-

At the Moor south wall, guide Paul Etter puts his hook into the wall. His foot is resting in a ladder, which is indispensable in such difficult terrain. His elegant posture does not show how strenuous it is to overcome such steep walls.

One of the most magnificent sections of the Alps as seen from an airplane: on the left, the mighty Weisshorn (4,505 meters) with its long northern edge, and the steep Schali ridge which plunges down to the Schali saddle. At the top to the right, the Matterhorn with its gloomy north wall. Almost below the Matterhorn peak, the jagged rocky edge of the Zinalrothorn. To its right, the Obergabelhorn with its steep, trapezoidal ice field, which can be seen from afar. At the top to the left, the Zermatt Breithorn, the Little Matterhorn, and the Theodul Pass.

The evening sky is reflected in the shiny surface of the Lago di Saoseo in the Val di Campo. This side valley of the Puschlav with its clear mountain lakes embedded in dark pine forests belongs to the most impressive natural beauties of Switzerland.

nance of club shelters and other club activities—such as tours, lectures, publications—the Swiss Alpenclub contributed a great deal towards the popularization of mountain climbing.

Almost all the high peaks of the Alps had been climbed by that time. Only the unfriendly Dent du Géant of the Montblanc massif soared unconquered into the sky and was left for the ambitious climber. In 1882 it was finally conquered with rope and picks by the Sella brothers from Biella and W. Graham and J. Joseph Maquignaz from Breuil. For the men of the Alpine Club, the Swiss mountains had lost some of their attraction. New and higher mountains were now the target—the Caucasus, the Himalayas, the Andes.

In the Alps a detailed exploration began. More and more difficult ascents were ventured. Englishman A. F. Mummery (1856–1895) was a very muscular man with an extraordinary strength of will who was not satisfied with a repetition of normal ascents to normal peaks. On September 3, 1879 he climbed the Matterhorn via the Zmutt Ridge together with Alexander Burgener, the famous guide from the Saas Valley, and Johann Petrus and Augustin Gentinetta. A year later he tried, together with Burgener, the steepest of all the Matterhorn ridges, the Furggen Ridge.

Since it was impossible to proceed from the Furggen saddle, the roped party crossed the upper part of the east wall to the Hörnli Ridge, an undertaking which even today gives goose pimples to any connoisseur of the Matterhorn. A. F. Mummery and Alexander Burgener were first-class experts at rock climbing. The rough towers and pins on the Montblanc were exactly to their liking. There was plenty of new territory for them. In 1880 they reached, together with B. Venetz, the Aiguille des Charmoz, and a year later the rocky tower of the Grépon. Mummery defended rock climbing: "Certainly it does not make much sense to refuse to call someone a mountaineer if he is capable of finding his way in difficult mountain terrain. It is against all laws of logic if it is maintained that people who climb because they love mountain climbing are not mountaineers, while others who do the same thing but have a scientific purpose deserve this title. I certainly admit that science has a greater social value than sport; however, that does not eliminate the fact that mountain climbing is a sport which cannot be changed by any method into geology, botany or topography. We are always reproached with the fact that our sport makes such fast technical progress—in my opinion, this cannot be appreciated enough."

More and more often Mummery went without a mountain guide. After extensive excursions into the Montblanc area, he went to the Caucasus, and in 1895 he disappeared on the Nanga Parbat.

So far the English had been the leaders in alpinism, but slowly this began to change. Salzburg professor Ludwig Purtscheller (1849–1900) was a phenomenon as far as collecting peaks is concerned.

He took extensive tours with the brothers Emil and Otto Zsigmondy; for instance, they traversed the Matterhorn, Rothorn and Weisshorn and the highest ice wall of the Alps, the east wall of the Monte Rosa. As Hans Mayer's companion, Purtscheller climbed the highest mountain in Africa, the Kibo, in 1889. In 1868 Berlin professor Paul Gussfeldt was the first German to stand on the peak of the Matterhorn. For five decades he climbed the Alps, often accompanied by guide Alexander Burgener. In 1878 Güssfeldt and guides Hans Grass and Joh. Gross were the first to succeed in overcoming the Bernina Notch. The ascent to the Pizzo Bianco and the traverse to the Bernina peak were very difficult and Güssfeldt does not recommend a repetition of this tour in his book, *In the High Alps.* "It is enough that someone found out how the Pizzo Bianco and the Piz Bernina are joined together; it is unnecessary to do this again." The famous Bianco ridge has meanwhile become one of the most popular tours in the high Alps. However, Gussfeldt has accomplished more difficult ascents. His greatest achievement was certainly the four-day crossing of the Peuterey Ridge on the Montblanc (8/14–17/1893) with guides Emile Rey from Courmayeur and Christian Klucker from Sils in the Fex Valley. This is the longest and most difficult crossing of a ridge in the Alps and is still today an extraordinary achievement.

Aside from Purtscheller, American William Augustus Brevoort Coolidge (1850–1926) was one of the best connoisseurs of the Alps during the late era of their discovery. Coolidge was first a parson in England but in 1896 he moved to Grindelwald in order to be always close to his beloved mountains. For seventeen years the great Christian Almer was his guide. During his long years as mountaineer he climbed 1,700 peaks and passes. His enterprising aunt, Miss Meta Brevoort, often accompanied him. She was the first woman to traverse the Matterhorn (1874) and also took part in the first climbing of the Jungfrau during winter. Besides his brave aunt, Coolidge's most faithful companion was four-legged—the dog Tschingel. Christian Almer had given the animal to his guests, who had given it the name of the first peak they climbed together—the Tschingelhorn. Tschingel became a great alpinist. The athletic dog participated in fifty-three tours of the high Alps, eleven of them first climbings. After the climbing of the Montblanc, the Alpine Club declared Tschingel an honorary member. Coolidge also became famous for his books on the Alps. The most important ones are *Josias Simler et les Origines de L'Alpinisme* and *The Alps in Nature and History.*

On June 22, 1896 Christian Almer and his wife celebrated their golden wedding anniversary on the peak of the Wetterhorn, a memorable family get-together and a remarkable achievement, especially for Mrs. Almer, who was not too used to mountain climbing. The idea for this "folly" came from thirty-one-year-old Andreas Fischer from Zaun near Meiringen. He came from a family of mountain guides. His godfather was the legendary mountain guide Melchior Anderegg. He was a successful man, first a teacher then doctor of literary science and, like his father, he was a mountain guide. Not only did he repeat the best tours in the Bern Highlands, where he lived, but he also explored the Alps from the Dauphiné to the Dolomites. Twice he participated in expeditions to the Caucasus.

In 1912 Andreas Fischer lost his life in a stormy night on the Aletschhorn. Andreas Fischer was a new type of mountain guide. He believed in the ideals of the mountain guide's tradition, but on the other hand, as an intellectual, he was able to inform the public of his knowledge, his experience and his feelings. His book, *Hiking in the High Mountains,* occupies an important place in alpine literature. Fischer's contemporary and the last true pioneer of mountain guides was Christian Klucker (1853–1928) from Sils in the Fex Valley. Klucker's specialty

30

was the granite mountains of the Bergell, where he succeeded in accomplishing dozens of first climbings. For the Englishmen, the somewhat hidden Bergell mountains were probably not high enough. Klucker was the first to awaken them from their sleeping-beauty rest. Today they and the Aiguilles of Chamonix are among the most beautiful primitive rock-terrains for climbers in the Alps. Klucker was a formidable rock climber, but he was also first-class on ice. He conquered the north wall of the Piz Roseg. Klucker became familiar with the entire Alps. In his *Memories of a Mountain Guide,* the list of his first climbings is four printed pages long.

During the last phase of the discovery period, the alpine skills in snow and ice became more and more refined. But there were still explorer-mountaineers who carried on the traditional exploration of the Alps as begun by the humanists. Geologist Albert Heim (1849–1937) spent a very rich lifework in the mountains, and so did botanist Carl Schröter (1855–1939). Eugéne Rambert (1830–1886), professor of literature from Lausanne, questioned the meaning of mountain climbing and found it in the spiritualization of experiencing nature. For decac' ₃ Heinrich Dübi (1848–1942) took care of the publications for the Swiss Alpenclub and he became a leading alpine historian.

The pioneers had conquered the alpine peaks and had made a breach in the psychological wall which had surrounded the mountains for a long time. Then came the masses, if not into the highest mountains, at least into the foothills of the Alps. Fast-developing technology contributed its share. In 1871 and 1874 the first Swiss mountain railroads started operation—the Rigi railroads of Vitznau and Arth. Enormous hotel buildings sprang up on the mountain, and from now on it was the duty of every tourist on an educational trip to admire a sunrise from the top of the Rigi. In 1888 the Pilatus railway followed and in 1892 the Brienzer-Rothorn and the Rochers-de-Naye railroads. In 1898 the rack-railway climbed up to the Gorner Ridge with its beautiful scenic view amidst the high

Standing on the Furka Pass one can see beyond the deep Wallis valley the highest peaks of Switzerland: the Monte Rosa massif whose Dufour Peak (4,634 meters) is the highest in Switzerland, the Mischabel Group, and the Dom (4,545 meters), the highest mountain which is located entirely in Switzerland, and the Weisshorn (4,505 meters).

31

mountains of 4,000 meters and more. In 1912 the absolute culmination was reached for decades to come with the construction of the Jungfrau railway to the 3,420-meter-high Jungfrau saddle. The first enthusiasm of technologically mastering the mountains would not stop before the highest peaks. Luckily, however, for future generations, technical and financial problems beset it. Therefore, we were spared a lift to the peak of the Jungfrau, and they still have not bored a tunnel through the Matterhorn, or chained it.

The period during which the more extensive mountain tours in the Alps can be undertaken under more or less normal circumstances is very short. It begins, at best, in June and lasts, at the most, until October—a total of four months! During winter the days are short and the nights are long, and ice and snow cause many problems. But in spite of this, many undaunted alpinists have tried to outdo winter.

Without skis and with equipment which today seems more funny than practical, Coolidge and his aunt, Miss Brevoort, guided by Almer, climbed the Jungfrau and the Wetterhorn in the middle of winter in 1874. In March of 1882 the great Italian mountain photographer Vittorio Sella and guides Jean-Antoine and Louis Carrel traversed the Matterhorn from Breuil to Zermatt, a difficult undertaking and a pioneer achievement of winter alpinism. During the short winter days Vittorio Sella liked the light and the clear views. His mountain pictures taken with a heavy plate camera are still unsurpassed today.

The English discovered that winter can be much more pleasant above the foggy valleys: "Oh, how the sunshine does me good! For weeks I lived in heavy fog and barbaric cold and up here there is brilliant sunshine which makes the temperatures of four or five degrees below zero feel like spring weather. In the Boss brothers' 'Bear' there is cozy British family life—the winter hotel is full of English tourists who pass their time sledding and skating." This is how Zürich alpinist C. Seeling starts his description of the climbing of the Mönch from Grindelwald in 1890. Englishmen are the greatest worshippers of the winter sun; however, until the discovery of skis, mountain tours during winter were restricted to a very small elite of mountain climbers. When snowshoes, which had been known by Lapps in Northern Europe for a long time, came into use, winter tourism in the Alps was not the same anymore. In 1883 Wilhelm Paulcke first experimented with "gliding woods" in Davos. At the same time the canons on the Great St. Bernhard tried skis. A sensation came in 1888—Norwegian Fridjof Nansen crossed Greenland on skis in forty days. Sceptics warned against using skis in the Alps even though they were quite useful on the highlands of Greenland and Lapland.

In 1891 the first alpine ski club was founded in Vienna. As early as 1894 various alpine passes—Gotthard, Furka, Grimsel and Bernia—were crossed on skis. In the same winter Carl Egger and Dr. Staübli climbed the first high peak

32

A roped party of three on the snow of the north ridge of the Weisshorn. Shortly after midnight the mountain guides left the Tracuit shelter (3,256 meters) and climbed across the Turtmann glacier to the Bishorn (4,159 meters). There the long and exposed path begins across the northern ridge to the Weisshorn peak (4,505 meters). Crampons make walking on the snow possible and there is no need to carve out steps.

on skis, the 2,985-meter-high Rothorn near Arosa. However, the skiing method of the Northerners was not satisfactory in the Alps. Austrian Mathias Zdarsky advocated a method adapted to alpine conditions which he named after his home town, the "Lilienfeld Ski Method". Georg Bilgeri tried to combine the advantages of the Norwegian with those of the Lilienfeld method. Ski clubs sprang up like mushrooms and the first ski instruction books appeared on the market. In 1896 Wilhelm Paulcke and Victor de Beauclair reached the peak of the Oberalpstock on skis—the first 3,000-meter ski mountain!

Now the conquest of the high mountains during winter really started. In 1898 Oskar Schuster used skis when climbing the Dufour peak, and in 1901 Henry Hoek reached the top of the Finsteraarhorn on skis. But skis did not remain simply a means of getting about the wintry mountains for long. The rapture of moving fast and the beauty of the alpine world in winter helped develop a sport which we all know today. Millions of sport enthusiasts now ski the Alps. Economywise, winter tourism has already far surpassed summer tourism. Gondolas and ski lifts have become so numerous in the Alps during the short history of skiing that lovers of the quiet world of the mountains have to escape into the last corners of the Alps. But the unspoiled beauty of the wintry mountains is revealed to the ski alpinist who can still find the solitude of the pioneer days, far away from ski lifts and trails.

At the beginning of the First World War the discovery period of the Swiss mountains came to a temporary close. The great economic crisis between the two World Wars (1918–1939) also cast its shadows on mountain tourism.

Rock climbing on the jagged peaks of the north edge of the Weisshorn. The most difficult part is on the Big Gendarm (to the right): a vertical chimney closed off by an overhanging rock. This ridge was first climbed by Hans Biehly and guide Heinrich Burgener on September 21, 1898.

In alpinism the time of the "last problems" had arrived. In 1921 the Mittellegi Ridge on the Eiger was conquered by a Japanese climber, Yukoh Maki, with guides Fritz Steuri, Samuel Brawand and Fritz Amatter, and an abundance of rope and hooks. Willo Welzenbach from Munich revolutionized the ice technique and with his companions climbed a number of tall north walls, e. g., in 1925 the north wall of the Dent d'Herens. In 1931 the brothers Franz and Toni Schmid rode their bicycles from Munich to Zermatt and were the first to climb the dark north wall of the Matterhorn. A year later, on August 20, 1932, the

incredibly steep 1,700-meter-high northeast wall of the Eiger was mastered. Dr. Hans Lauper and Alfred Zürcher climbed this wall under the expert guidance of Josef Knubel and Alexander Graven.

As early as 1923 Alfred Zürcher, together with mountain guide Walter Risch, had opened an elegant climbing route in the Bergell—the 800-meter-high north edge of the Piz Badile. In 1935 the brothers Alfred and Otto Amstad and Guido Masetto succeeded in climbing the difficult southern ridge of the Salbitschijen. From July 21–24, 1938 the direct north wall of the Eiger, which had been courted for years, was mastered by Anderl Heckmaier and Ludwig Voerg from Munich and Fritz Kasparek and Heinrich Harrer from Vienna.

On September 26, 1938 guide Hermann Steuri and Miss Lüthy and Hans Haidegger found a difficult path across the 700-meter-high east wall of the Kingspitz.

For the average mountaineer, all the paths had long been mapped out. But still—is not every ascent which is done for the first time something like a personal first climbing?

However, the extremists among the mountain climbers still found enough to do after the First World War. Only then were the southern slopes of the Churfirsten, which are ideal for climbing, discovered.

The mountain climber's equipment has improved. The spiked shoe disappeared; the profiled rubber sole proved to be good in every terrain. Heavy-duty climbing boots have steel or plastic supports which facilitate standing on the smallest footholds. Added to the ordinary assortment of hooks was a special hook which allowed the climbing of solid, completely crackless rocks. Stepladders are part of the standard equipment of the rock climber because on very difficult terrain they do not only have to climb vertical, but also overhanging rocks. Light and yet protective camping gear made of plastic and down facilitate

There is snow on the north ridge of the Weisshorn between the peak and the Big Gendarm (4,331 meters). Often there are snowdrifts. The mountaineer walks a ridge of weird beauty.

35

climbing in winter, which has become very popular. Masses of tourists spend their winter vacation on the ski trails; ski tours in the high mountains are made by thousands. But climbing difficult terrain during adverse winter conditions—that is a task for pioneers only. From March 6–12, 1961 Walter Almberger, Toni Hiebeler, Toni Kinshofer and Anderl Mannhart fought their way through the wintry north wall of the Eiger. In February 1962 two guides, Hilty von Almen and Paul Etter, climbed the north wall of the Matterhorn during an Arctic cold wave. Ice, storm and cold made these undertakings even more difficult. In one respect winter had its advantages—there were no falling rocks or ice. Each route, no matter how difficult, is now climbed in winter—a new kind of alpinism which is not always convincing.

The mountaineers have to watch the calendar—a tour under excellent conditions in February is still winter climbing and, therefore, connected with considerable prestige. An ascent in April during masses of new snow and great cold is not considered more impressive than any other summer tour. So far the most extraordinary alpinistic feats were accomplished on the Eiger wall. Equipped for an expedition (600 hooks, 1,500 meters of rope, and one month's time), Douglas Haston and his companions defied the Eiger in March 1966 and found a new direct route on the north wall. American John Harlin fell to his death during the ascent. Three years later, on August 15, 1969, after one month's work, Japanese climbers T. and Y. Kato, S. Negishi, H. Amano, S. Kubo and Michiko Imai reached the Eiger peak on a new *super-direttissima* (very direct route). The number of adventurers in rock and ice climbing is rising.

Former generations would never have dreamed of how busy the Alps are today. The once isolated mountains are "explored" from slope to slope, from top to bottom, by cable cars, ski lifts, Alpine flights, construction of roads and power stations. And with more technology, more and more people come. Do they come in search of fresh air, mountain peace and clean brooks? Then it is time that we try to preserve what is left of the peace and solitude of the Alps. The space of the Alps is limited too.

Already the environmental problems of the more populated areas are a danger to the Alps. It is to be hoped that regional planning and environmental protection, which are slowly coming into action, will prevent the worst. It would be so nice if we could still show our children and our children's children a little bit of the genuine alpine world, and if Friedrich von Tschudi's statement could still be valid today—that the Alps are the pride of the Swiss.

Edward Whymper (1840–1911) The English illustrator first came into contact with the mountains because he had to illustrate a book for his publisher. He later became world-famous as the first to climb the Matterhorn. In his book, Scrambles Amongst the Alps, *he describes the climb. His description is one of the most gripping in alpine literature, and stands in the first rank of adventure stories. Even today it has not lost any of its excitement and immediacy.*

3 EDWARD WHYMPER
The First Ascent of the Matterhorn

We started from Zermatt on the 13th of July 1865, at half-past five, on a brilliant and perfectly cloudless morning. We were eight in number—Croz, old Peter and his two sons, Lord F. Douglas, Hadow, Hudson, and I. To ensure steady motion, one tourist and one native walked together. The youngest Taugwalder fell to my share, and the lad marched well, proud to be on the expedition, and happy to show his powers. The wine-bags also fell to my lot to carry, and throughout the day, after each drink, I replenished them secretly with water, so that at the next halt they were found fuller than before! This was considered a good omen, and little short of miraculous.

On the first day we did not intend to ascend to any great height, and we mounted, accordingly, very leisurely; picked up the things which were left in the chapel at the Schwarzsee at 8:20, and proceeded thence along the ridge connecting the Hörnli with the Matterhorn. At half-past eleven we arrived at the base of the actual peak; then quitted the ridge, and clambered round some ledges, on to the eastern face. We were now fairly upon the mountain, and were astonished to find that places which from the Riffel, or even from the Furggen Glacier, looked entirely impracticable, were so easy that we could *run about.*

Before twelve o'clock we had found a good position for the tent, at a height of 11,000 feet. Croz and young Peter went on to see what was above, in order to save time on the following morning. They cut across the heads of the snow-slopes which descended towards the Furggen Glacier, and disappeared round a corner; but shortly afterwards we saw them high up on the face, moving quickly. We others made a solid platform for the tent in a well-protected spot, and then watched eagerly for the return of the men. The stones which they upset told us that they were very high, and we supposed that the way must be easy. At length, just before 3 p.m., we saw them coming down, evidently much excited. "What are they saying, Peter?" "Gentlemen, they say it is no good." But when they came near we heard a different story. "Nothing but what was good; not a difficulty, not

a single difficulty! We could have gone to the summit and returned to-day easily!"

We passed the remaining hours of daylight—some basking in the sunshine, some sketching or collecting; and when the sun went down, giving, as it departed, a glorious promise for the morrow, we returned to the tent to arrange for the night. Hudson made tea, I coffee, and we then retired each one to his blanket bag; the Taugwalders, Lord Francis Douglas, and myself, occupying the tent, the others remaining, by preference, outside. Long after dusk the cliffs above echoed with our laughter and with the songs of the guides, for we were happy that night in camp, and feared no evil.

We assembled together outside the tent before dawn on the morning of the 14th, and started directly it was light enough to move. Young Peter came on with us as a guide, and his brother returned to Zermatt. We followed the route which had been taken on the previous day, and in a few minutes turned the rib which had intercepted the view of the eastern face from our tent platform. The whole of this great slope was now revealed, rising for 3,000 feet like a huge natural staircase. Some parts were more, and others were less, easy; but we were not once brought to a halt by any serious impediment, for when an obstruction was met in front it could always be turned to the right or the left. For the greater part of the way there was, indeed, no occasion for the rope, and sometimes Hudson led, sometimes myself. At 6.20 we had attained a height of 12,800 feet, and halted for half an hour; we then continued the ascent without a break until 9.55, when stopped for fifty minutes, at a height of 14,000 feet. Twice we struck the north-east ridge and followed it for some little distance,—to no advantage, for it was usually more rotten and steep, and always more difficult than the face.[1] Still, we kept to it, lest stones perchance might fall.

We had now arrived at the foot of that part which, from the Riffelberg or from Zermatt, seems perpendicular or overhanging, and could no longer contin-

Cembra pine on Engstlen Lake. The Titlis group in the background. Like no other tree, the Cembra pine has become a symbol
of the desolate regions of the mountains. Alone and in groups, it
winds or wraps its strong roots around the bare rocks and
through centuries defies storms and avalanches.

ue upon the eastern side. For a little distance we ascended by snow upon the arête—that is, the ridge—descending towards Zermatt, and then, by common consent, turned over to the right, or to the northern side. Before doing so, we made a change in the order of ascent. Croz went first, I followed, Hudson came third; Hadow and old Peter were last. "Now," said Croz, as he led off, "now for something altogether different." The work became difficult and required caution. In some places there was little to hold, and it was desirable that those should be in front who were least likely to slip. The general slope of the mountain at this part was *less* than 40°, and snow had accumulated in, and had filled up, the interstices of the rock-face, leaving only occasional fragments projecting here and there. These were at times covered with a thin film of ice, produced from the melting and refreezing of the snow. It was the counterpart, on a small scale, of the upper 700 feet of the Pointe des Ecrins,—only there was this material difference; the face of the Ecrins was about, or exceeded, an angle of 50°, and the Matterhorn face was less than 40°. It was a place over which any fair mountaineer might pass in safety, and Mr. Hudson ascended this part, and, as far as I know, the entire mountain, without having the slightest assistance rendered to him upon any occasion. Sometimes, after I had taken a hand from Croz, or received a pull, I turned to offer the same to Hudson; but he invariably declined, saying it was not necessary. Mr. Hadow, however, was not accustomed to this kind of work, and required continual assistance. . . . The difficulty which he found at this part arose simply and entirely from want of experience.

This solitary difficult part was of no great extent. We bore away over it at first, nearly horizontally, for a distance of about 400 feet; then ascended directly towards the summit for about 60 feet; and then doubled back to the ridge which descends towards Zermatt. A long stride round a rather awkward corner brought us to snow once more. The last doubt vanished! The Matterhorn was ours! Nothing but 200 feet of easy snow remained to be surmounted!

You must now carry your thoughts back to the seven Italians who started from Breuil on the 11th of July. Four days had passed since their departure, and we were tormented with anxiety lest they should arrive on the top before us. All the way up we had talked of them, and many false alarms of "men on the summit" had been raised. The higher we rose, the more intense became the excitement. What if we should be beaten at the last moment? The slope eased off, at length we could be detached, and Croz and I, dashing away, ran a neck-and-neck race, which ended in a dead heat. At 1:40 p.m. the world was at our feet, and the Matterhorn was conquered. Hurrah! Not a footstep could be seen.

It was not yet certain that we had not been beaten. The summit of the Matterhorn was formed of a rudely level ridge, about 350 feet long, and the Italians might have been at its farther extremity. I hastened to the southern end, scanning the snow right and left eagerly. Hurrah! again; it was untrodden. "Where were the men?" I peered over the cliff, half doubting, half expectant, and saw them immediately—mere dots on the ridge, at an immense distance below. Up went my arms and my hat. "Croz! Croz!! come here!" "Where are they, Monsieur?" "There, don't you see them, down there?" "Ah! the *coquins*, they are low down." "Croz, we must make those fellows hear us." We yelled until we were hoarse. The Italians seemed to regard us—we could not be certain. "Croz, we *must* make them hear us; they *shall* hear us!" I seized a block of rock and hurled it down, and called upon my companion, in the name of friendship, to do the same. We drove our sticks in, and prized away the crags, and soon a torrent of stones poured down the cliffs. There was no mistake about it this time. The Italians turned and fled.

Still, I would that the leader of that party could have stood with us at that moment, for our victorious shouts conveyed to him the disappointment of the ambition of a lifetime. He was *the* man, of all those who attempted the ascent of the Matterhorn, who most deserved to be the first upon its summit. He was the first to doubt its inaccessibility, and he was the only man who persisted in believing that its ascent would be accomplished. It was the aim of his life to make the ascent from the side of Italy, for the honour of his native valley. For a time he had the game in his hands: he played it as he thought best; but he made a false move, and he lost it.

The others had arrived, so we went back to the northern end of the ridge. Croz now took the tent-pole, and planted it in the highest snow. "Yes," we said, "there is the flag-staff, but where is the flag?" "Here it is," he answered, pulling off his blouse and fixing it to the stick. It made a poor flag, and there was no wind to float it out, yet it was seen all around. They saw it at Zermatt—at the Riffel—in the Val Tournanche. At Breuil, the watchers cried, "Victory is ours!" They raised "bravos" for Carrel, and "vivas" for Italy, and hastened to put themselves *en fête*. On the morrow they were undeceived. "All was changed; the explorers returned sad—cast down—disheartened—confounded—gloomy." "It is true,"

said the men. "We saw them ourselves—they hurled stones at us! The old traditions *are* true,—there are spirits on the top of the Matterhorn!"

We returned to the southern end of the ridge to build a cairn, and then paid homage to the view. The day was one of those superlatively calm and clear ones which usually precede bad weather. The atmosphere was perfectly still, and free from all clouds or vapours. Mountains fifty—nay a hundred—miles off, looked sharp and near. All their details—ridge and crag, snow and glacier—stood out with faultless definition. Pleasant thoughts of happy days in bygone years came up unbidden, as we recognized the old, familiar forms. All were revealed—not one of the principal peaks of the Alps was hidden. I see them clearly now—the great inner circles of giants, backed by the ranges, chains, and *massifs*. First came the Dent Blanche, hoary and grand; the Gabelhorn and pointed Rothorn; and then the peerless Weisshorn: the towering Mischabelhörner, flanked by the Allalinhorn, Strahlhorn, and Rimpfischhorn; then Monte Rosa—with its many Spitzes—the Lyskamm and the Breithorn. Behind were the Bernese Oberland, governed by the Finsteraarhorn; the Simplon and St. Gotthard groups; the Disgrazia and the Ortler. Towards the south we looked down to Chivasso on the plain of Piedmont, and far beyond. The Viso—one hundred miles away— seemed close upon us; the Maritime Alps—one hundred and thirty miles distant —were free from haze. Then came my first love—the Pelvoux; the Ecrins and the Meije; the clusters of the Graians; and lastly, in the west, glowing in full sunlight, rose the monarch of all—Mont Blanc. Ten thousand feet beneath us were the green fields of Zermatt, dotted with chalets, from which blue smoke rose lazily. Eight thousand feet below, on the other side, were the pastures of Breuil. There were forests black and gloomy, and meadows bright and lively; bounding waterfalls and tranquil lakes; fertile lands and savage wastes; sunny plains and frigid *plateaux*. There were the most rugged forms, and the most

42

Game—goats, fawns and young bucks—in the steep rocks of the Alpstein. Ignorance and superstition almost completely destroyed the ibex in the Swiss Alps during the last centuries. On May 8, 1911 the first purebred animals were set free in the Highlands of St. Gallen. Their naturalization was successful. In 1965 approximately 3,700 animals lived in more than forty colonies.

Chamoix in the Calfeisen Valley. The game has a hard time in the mountains during winter. Weak or sick animals have not much of a chance to survive. It is difficult to find food. As long as the snow is soft the animals can scrape for old grass under the snow. The formation of ice and crusty snow after a warm spell is devastating for the game.

graceful outlines—bold, perpendicular cliffs, and gentle undulating slopes; rocky mountains and snowy mountains, sombre and solemn, or glittering and white, with walls—turrets—pinnacles—pyramids—domes—cones—and spires! There was every combination that the world can give, and every contrast that the heart could desire.

We remained on the summit for one hour—

One crowded hour of glorious life.

It passed away too quickly, and we began to prepare for the descent.

Hudson and I again consulted as to the best and safest arrangement of the

44

An avalanche falls down the steep slope of the Orglen in the Calfeisen Valley. This valley has many avalanches. Much game spends the winter here, and even though the animals have a keen sense of the danger, in almost every winter dozens of them are buried under the snow.

party. We agreed that it would be best for Croz to go first, and Hadow second; Hudson, who was almost equal to a born mountaineer in sureness of foot, wished to be third; Lord Francis Douglas was placed next, and old Peter, the strongest of the remainder, after him. I suggested to Hudson that we should attach a rope to the rocks on our arrival at the difficult bit, and hold it as we descended, as an additional protection. He approved the idea, but it was not definitely settled that it should be done. The party was being arranged in the above order whilst I was sketching the summit, and they had finished, and were waiting for me to be tied in line, when someone remembered that our names had not been left in a bottle. They requested me to write them down, and moved off while it was being done.

A few minutes afterwards I tied myself to young Peter, ran down after the others, and caught them just as they were commencing the descent of the difficult part. Great care was being taken. Only one man was moving at a time; when he was firmly planted the next advanced, and so on. They had not, however, attached the additional rope to rocks, and nothing was said about it. The suggestion was not made for my own sake, and I am not sure that it even occurred to me again. For some little distance we two followed the others, detached from them, and should have continued so had not Lord Francis Douglas asked me, about 3 p.m., to tie on to old Peter, as he feared, he said, that Taugwalder would not be able to hold his ground if a slip occurred.

A few minutes later, a sharp-eyed lad ran into the Monte Rosa Hotel, to Seiler, saying that he had seen an avalanche fall from the summit of the Matterhorn on to the Matterhorn Glacier. The boy was reproved for telling idle stories; he was right, nevertheless, and this was what he saw.

Michel Croz had laid aside his axe, and in order to give Mr. Hadow greater security, was absolutely taking hold of his legs, and putting his feet, one by one, into their proper positions. So far as I know, no one was actually descending. I cannot speak with certainty, because the two leading men was partially hidden from my sight by an intervening mass of rock, but it is my belief, from the movements of their shoulders, that Croz, having done as I have said, was in the act of turning round, to go down a step or two himself; at this moment Mr. Hadow slipped, fell against him, and knocked him over. I heard one startled exclamation from Croz, then saw him and Mr. Hadow flying downwards; in another moment Hudson was dragged from his steps, and Lord Francis Douglas immediately after him. All this was the work of a moment. Immediately we heard Croz's exclamation, old Peter and I planted ourselves as firmly as the rocks would permit: the rope was taut between us, and the jerk came on us both as on one man. We held; but the rope broke midway between Taugwalder and Lord Francis Douglas. For a few seconds we saw our unfortunate companions sliding downwards on their backs, and spreading out their hands, endeavouring to save themselves. They passed from our sight uninjured, disappeared one by one, and fell from precipice to precipice on the Matterhorn Glacier below, a distance of

46

nearly 4,000 feet in height. From the moment the rope broke it was impossible to help them.

So perished our comrades! For the space of half an hour we remained on the spot without moving a single step. The two men, paralysed by terror, cried like infants, and trembled in such a manner as to threaten us with the fate of the others. Old Peter rent the air with exclamations of "Chamonix! Oh, what will Chamonix say?" He meant, Who would believe that Croz could fall? The young man did nothing but scream or sob, "We are lost! we are lost!" Fixed between the two, I could neither move up nor down. I begged young Peter to descend, but he dared not. Unless he did, we could not advance. Old Peter became alive to the danger, and swelled the cry, "We are lost! we are lost!" The father's fear was natural—he trembled for his son; the young man's fear was cowardly—he thought of self alone. At last old Peter summoned up courage, and changed his position to a rock to which he could fix the rope; the young man then descended, and we all stood together. Immediately we did so, I asked for the rope which had given way, and found, to my surprise—indeed, to my horror—that it was the weakest of the three ropes. It was not brought, and should not have been employed, for the purpose for which it was used. It was old rope, and, compared with the others, was feeble. It was intended as a reserve, in case we had to leave much rope behind, attached to rocks. I saw at once that a serious question was involved, and made him give me the end. It had broken in midair, and it did not appear to have sustained previous injury.

For more than two hours afterwards I thought almost every moment that the next would be my last; for the Taugwalders, utterly unnerved, were not only incapable of giving assistance, but were in such a state that a slip might have been expected from them at any moment. After a time, we were able to do that which should have been done at first, and fixed rope to firm rocks, in addition to being tied together. These ropes were cut from time to time, and were left behind.

The Engadin Dolomites are not attractive for the accomplished alpinist but they are very suitable for hiking in the mountains. From Piz Lischanna (3,105 meters) across Schuls one can see the Ortler and the numerous peaks of the eastern Alps on clear autumn days.

47

Even with their assurance the men were afraid to proceed, and several times old Peter turned with ashy face and faltering limbs, and said, with terrible emphasis, "*I cannot!*"

About 6 p.m. we arrived at the snow upon the ridge descending towards Zermatt, and all peril was over. We frequently looked, but in vain, for traces of our unfortunate companions; we bent over the ridge and cried to them, but no sound returned. Convinced at last that they were neither within sight nor hearing, we ceased from our useless efforts; and, too cast down for speech, silently gathered up our things, and the little effects of those who were lost, preparatory to continuing the descent. When, lo! a mighty arch appeared, rising above the Lyskamm, high into the sky. Pale, colourless, and noiseless, but perfectly sharp and defined, except where it was lost in the clouds, this unearthly apparition seemed like a vision from another world; and, almost appalled, we watched with amazement the gradual development of two vast crosses, one on either side. If the Taugwalders had not been the first to perceive it, I should have doubted my senses. They thought it had some connection with the accident, and I, after a while, that it might bear some relation to ourselves. But our movements had no effect upon it. The spectral forms remained motionless. It was a fearful and wonderful sight; unique in my experience, and impressive beyond description, coming at such a moment.

Jules Michelet (1798–1874) The French historian, philosopher, and author was an idol of the youth of his time and an enthusiastic fighter for truth and democracy. As with Rousseau, idealistic presentations of society were intermixed with love for the beauties of nature. This wonderful section about Alpine trees comes from Michelet's La Montagne.

4   JULES MICHELET
The Trees of the Alps

One is wholly unable to disembarrass oneself of an emotion of gratitude and religious reverence when, wandering alone among the elevated pasturages of Switzerland, one encounters some of these venerable firs which for ages have been preserved as a refuge and a protection for the herd. One perceives in such localities the importance of the tree's mission. One feels that it is the friend and protector of all life. And well does every creature know it; goats, and sheep, and lambs, and indolent cows, spontaneously resort to its shade to enjoy their repose, each perfectly well acquainted with its own *gogant*—(the name borne by these protecting trees in the Pays de Vaud). There they establish themselves in the summertime, and are at home. Near at hand the cascade murmurs. At different stages of the lofty tree buzzes and swarms a world of squirrels, insects, and birds. All around and about it, at a few paces distant, in the warm sunshine and defended from the wind, flourishes many a charming plant excluded from the fields, and harshly spurned by the labourer as a worthless herb. But the tree forbids nothing. It is the common father of all; it is, as it were, the good genius of the land. . . .

The whole life of the country has centred in two trees: the heroic and vigorous arolla, which, if left to itself, would endure almost for ever; and the smiling larch, incessantly renewed, and with its yearly verdure simulating eternal youth.

Both are supported, in these severe regions, by a miracle of nature which requires explanation. Heat and life are cherished, guarded, and concentrated in them—are impenetrably shut in—by an internal defence, which is as good as a house, and which, in the bitterest winter, preserves for them the *home*. This defence is—the resin. . . .

This resin resists the cold in three ways. First, it acts as a solder. Then, owing to its density and thickness, it does not freeze. Finally, as carbon, it is a non-

49

conductor of heat, and, far from permitting it to escape, preserves and concentrates it within. . . .

The finest of all resins is that of the larch, which in commerce is known as Venetian turpentine—a substance of astonishing subtlety, and exceeding penetrability. An atom introduced into any living organism penetrates it immediately, and traverses the entire course of its circulation.

In all the arts these resins have proved of the greatest utility. Every painter has need of them. And even the musician uses them for his stringed instruments, and by their means makes his bow vibrate.

But is not the tree itself an instrument? One is surprised to see, in the cold Engadine, the interior of the larch exhibiting those warm hues which render the violin so pleasant in the eyes of colourists. Like the Alpine flowers, it absorbs the living light, and thence derives that fine red tone which one might suppose to be its youthful blood. . . .

With respect to its seeds it acts very wisely. Though they are ripe in autumn, it retains and guards them, nor ventures to let them forth until the spring. With this pledge of the future shut up and concentrated within itself, abandoning to the wind its thenceforth useless leaves, it bends before the hissing and raging gale, when stimulated into action by the winter. Its bare branches, affording little hold to the wind, come and go, and resist it all the more successfully that they do not offer any virtual resistance.

Far from exhausting itself by reproducing its leaves, it converts them into myriads of nourishing agents, which augment its sap and increase its vitality. And therefore it seems to be always young, a stranger to the country, the offspring of a happier clime. . . .

It is the hope and the joy of the mountain. It labours incessantly to re-create the forest. But the more it accomplishes, the more is demanded of it. It supplies the thousand wants of the country. Whence come those ceilings? From the larch. What builds up yonder noble and imposing grange? Again, the larch. Its beautiful, odorous wood, worthy of the highest artistic purposes, is wastefully expended upon the hearth. . . .

Only one being has the right to plant itself on the brink of the glacier. One alone can contemplate it face to face, through the long ten months of winter, and not perish. The winter cleaves the stone, but the tree laughs at its fury. The winter maddens and rages, but cannot subdue the tree's profound and vigorous vitality. The winds rush to the assault; the furious hurricanes heap up the mass of snows, and overwhelm everything, except the arolla. It has the royal privilege of never carrying a burthen. You see it speedily emerging from the snow, rising above it, and flinging it off its vigorous arms. It reappears with tranquil front, and raises heavenward its magnificent lustres; each of which is adorned with a lofty plume of leaves.

On the ascent to the glacier, the effect is impressive. All life gradually dimin-

50

Autumn Lärch trees in the lower region. As beautiful as a heavenly church window, the glowing tree appears before the dark-shadowed valley ground. When the autumn night frosts have destroyed the last floral splendor along the mountain paths, the Lärch trees begin changing colors and blooming for the last time in many mountain regions. It is as if nature would once again condense her entire splendor of colors before the desolation of winter.

ishes. The great trees are dwarfed, to live as humble and feeble coppices. The birch-tree of the far North—of Russia—that stout friend of the frost and rime, before the wild demon, the ferocity of the glacier, grows afraid, and lowers its crest. Yet, on the very edge you see the arolla, in its tallest stature, in its fulness of life, untouched and unchanged. On the sheltered slopes it may be seen languishing, overloaded with lichens. But here, in the face of the terrible winds, and the midst of the mighty struggle, it flings off its garb of dree. Naked, like a skilled athlete, grasping the bare rock with its strong roots, it awaits the avalanche,—unconquerable and superb,—rearing aloft its conquering arms, and in these regions of death bearing witness to everlasting life. . . .

The ages being all its own, it is in no hurry. It does little, but does that little well. It slowly elaborates its admirable wood, and brings it to perfection. To accomplish its full growth it requires a thousand years. . . .

To wound the arolla is a crime, for it is the only tree which one cannot renew.

Who will plant it, when, in the course of a hundred years, it does not acquire the thickness of a man's fist? In our hurried and utilitarian epoch, who will give any thoughts to future generations?

But, on the other hand, you may seek in vain to replace the arolla; in vain attempt it with the light (and soulless) birch, or the other meagre trees of the North. They are all powerless here. The glacier reduces them to the condition of dwarfs and abortions. But the sun is specially fatal and terrible to them; at certain times, it can annihilate them with a glance.

The arolla struggles and holds its ground successfully against both enemies, the sharp javelin of the frost, the overpowering sun. Since the Alps were Alps, it has defended the mountain against the two destroyers.

The misfortune of the arolla is that of all heroes. So brave against the blows of Fate—living so hard a life of trial and combat—it preserves, nevertheless, a tender heart. It is vulnerable from within. Its fragrant pleasant wood, of so fine and regular a texture, has the grave misfortune of being wholly free from defect, of being very easily wrought. It is cut without difficulty, and carved with the

Fire Lilies in the "Val della Porta" in Tessin. They stand here representative of all the splendor of the mountain flowers that enchant the wanderers and mountain climbers from the valley to the highest heights.

The clear water of the Murg Brook plunges over an overgrown, rocky step. The water is gathered from the Murg Ponds throughout the Murg Valley in the Walensee. It is a brook of strength and a frothy love of life, nowhere tapped and pressed into pipes and tubes— a brook which, unfortunately, is too uncommon in the Alps.

utmost ease. Hence a succession of sacrileges. An imbecile shepherd, with his rude knife, cuts out of this age-old timber ridiculous images of sheep and grotesque goats, which are sold at Vienna, at Nuremburg, and on the Rhine. Tomorrow the foolish mother of this destructive child gives out the mighty heart which defended the Alps, to be used as a doll, dismembered, flung aside, and burned!

It is a sacred palladium. Living in it, the country maintains itself and maintains its own life. Dying, it also dies, perishes little by little, and when the last tree is cut, the last man will disappear.

Friedrich von Tschudi (1820–1886) The Swiss scholar, writer, and statesman, was at first a pastor in Lichtensteig. Because of failing health, he resigned in 1847 and moved as an independent scholar to St. Gallen. There he wrote his book Animal Life in the Alps. *It was published in 1853 in Leipzig for the first time, and from then on, many new editions and translations followed, far into our own century. Tschudi's linguistically masterful animal portrayals are the fruit of long observations of nature, which so far have not been surpassed. In his later years, Tschudi became administrative adviser and representative of St. Gallen.*

5 FRIEDRICH VON TSCHUDI
About Chamois and Marmots

The chamois are, above all other animals of the Alps, the most beloved of the alpine wanderers. Whether one sees them resting inoffensively in the most remote valleys under the protection of their guard, or, when unexpectedly surprised, retreating uphill like shadows over steep slopes and cliffs, quick as lightning and as though carried by winds, one's eyes always follow these charming creatures with deep interest. Like a personification of freedom, they know how to resist stubbornly thousands of dangers in a hard struggle. As is commonly known, the chamois very much resembles the goat, especially the alpine goat; but even from far away it differs from the goat by its extremely tough, twelve-to-twenty-seven-centimeter-long horns, which are curled at the bottom, notched, lengthwise round, pitch-black, and which recoil at the tip. Behind stand the pointed ears, which are turned forward when listening. It differs also by its longer and plumper legs, its craned neck and shorter and more compact frame. This is altogether resilient, and the neck is particularly extensible. Standing on all fours, it is able to stretch itself to a height of 180 centimeters while its weight rests almost entirely on its hind legs.

It has no beard like the capricorn's. Only in winter does it show a tinge of beard but this does not, in any case, justify those bad pictures which traditionally adorn it with a hardy goat's beard. In spring the chamois has the brightest color, brown-yellow; in summer it becomes fawn-colored, reddish-brown; in autumn it darkens to a brown-gray and becomes blackish brown-gray, sometimes even coal-black, in December. Only the dark stripe over the cheeks from eye to nose and the white-yellow parts on the nose, on the lower chin, on the forehead and on the belly, as well as the black-brown stripe on the back, remain the same in all coats.

The hair does not change every time with the coloring. It is probably the difference in nutriment, combined with atmospheric influences and the effect of

54

light, which alone determines the change in color. The fur is extremely thick in winter. The coarse and brittle upper hair grows to a length of sixteen centimeters in old rams, especially at the head, the abdomen and the feet; above the backbone in older animals, it often forms a mane with hair ten to twenty centimeters long. The feet of the chamois are much thicker than those of the goat and can (because its hoofs are provided, especially on the forefeet, with a horny encasement, hard as steel in front, rubber-like elastic in back) be spread wide, which proves to be very useful while walking over ice or on narrow rock ledges. Its track is similar to the goat's but somewhat more oblong, pointed and sharper, particularly in the outer hooves. The large, dark, strongly convex and lively shining eyes of this intelligent animal are of special beauty. The angle-like curved points of the horns, provided with indistinct bulges, are sharp and fine—superb weapons to defend against eagles and hawks and with which, when provoked, to quickly slit open the bellies of dogs. It really never fights man. The

Sunset in the towers and spikes of the Sciora range in Bergell. From left to right: Sciora Dafora (3,169 meters), Punta Pioda di Sciora (3,228 meters) Ago di Sciora (3,205 meters), and Sciora Dadent (3,275 meters). The first ascent of all four towers was executed by guide Christian Klucker from Fextal, together with guests, between 1888 and 1893. On August 2, 1923 guide Walter Risch, together with Alfred Zuercher, succeeded in crossing the entire range in one attempt.

Alpine guide Paul Etter demonstrates details of climbing techniques on large boulders behind the Sciora hut.

Aerial step over fissure. The climber whose path often leads over chasms cannot afford to become dizzy.

1. Wedging in the chimney.

Depending on the width of the chimney and height of the climber different methods are applied. Here the often-used technique: back towards the wall, feet against the opposite wall.

3. Overcoming a steep crack with the so-called Duelfer (layback) technique.

The hands grip the edge of the crack, the legs push against the slab. Duelfer was one of the pioneers of difficult rock climbing.

5. Traversing the rope in Duelfersitz.

Insurmountable rocks can be overcome by descent on rope. The mountaineer climbs as high as he can, traverses downward to a passable area from which he climbs up again. Duelfer's motto: you go as far as it goes and when it does not go, you traverse and keep on going.

2. Descent on double rope in Duelfersitz.

Overhangs and difficult rock are overcome in descent by roping down (abseiling). It is important to anchor the rope safely and make its retrieval possible.

4. Belaying the first climber.

The belayer is self-belayed on a solid rock. This belaying is the foundation of any further safety technique. Here the leader is protected by the dynamic belay (shoulder-and-spike) technique.

6. A simple down-roping (abseiling) method on not too steep slopes is the belly-brake. The climber stands between the two ropes, facing down, and descends by unwinding the one rope left and the other one right across the stomach.

ram, generally somewhat taller and more stubborn, has horns placed further apart and somewhat thicker than those of the female. Characteristic in the chamois is a rather large shell-like gland cavity behind each horn, which in rams during mating time swells up sponge-like similar to the eye-bulges of the copulating primeval cock, and disperses a permeating odor.

The usual summer abodes of the chamois are the impassable and highest areas of the high Alps up to the snow region. During this time they do not go into the valley unless they are dispersed. Yet one could, even a few years ago, when the mountains of the Glarnerland were still not frequented, see them at sunrise come down in small flocks and drink at the Sernf. In less protected regions they like to camp near the glaciers. At dawn and often during moonlit nights, they graze down on slopes or search for lower-lying grazing spots protected all around by rocks; they remain usually from nine o'clock to eleven o'clock at the rim of steeply sloping and lightly foliated rocks, rise again during midday, and graze slowly uphill. They rest, ruminating, till four o'clock on the shady side of rugged canyons, if possible close to snow, which they love. Often they linger for hours on bare glaciers and, in the evening, like to visit again the pastures of the morning. Nights are best spent in company under overhangs or between boulders. They seem to be gayest in late fall and early winter and during breeding time. Then we observed for hours whole herds, as well as single pairs, in zealous play and sham-fights. They roam around madly on the smallest mountain rims, endeavoring to throw each other off with their horns, pretending an attack on one place and at the same moment hurling themselves like lightning upon another; or they tease each other in a most mischievous manner. The moment they become aware of man, even from a remote distance, the scene changes immediately. All animals, from the oldest ram to the smallest kid, are at the look-out and are ready to escape. Even if the observer does not move an inch, the gay mood of the animals does not return. Slowly they move uphill, watching from every rock and every rim of an abyss, and they do not, even for a moment, lose sight of possible danger.

At the rim of the highest rock, the entire flock gathers closely together and

In spring, when the days are long and the glaciers are so covered with snow that snow bridges able to bear loads are covering the crevasses, it is time for alpine ski tours. A rope team of three—on glaciers three is the minimum—climbs between the ice towers to the twin glacier, the Castor (4,226 meters). Each year dozens of people lose their lives because of breaks in glacier crevasses, some only because they are not at all, or not properly, roped.

gazes endlessly into the depth, their white shining heads suspiciously and continuously moving to and fro. In summer one will not see these chamois again on the same day in this region; in autumn, on the other hand, and where the mountains are more solitary, they gallop down the slopes after about an hour and occupy their old playground.

We have noticed that in high summer they prefer the western and northern mountainsides; in all other seasons, rather the eastern and southern sides. Just as in the fall the snow turns the pinnacles of the Alps into silver and gradually goes down deeper into the pastures, so the chamois, too, withdraw farther to the higher mountain forests, till they have settled there in their final base camp for the winter. For such they like to choose the southern side of the mountains, often near the bare and steep slopes, from which the wind has cleared the snow. The umbrella or weather pines, whose arms hang down almost to the ground, protecting the long arid grass from snow, are preferred above any other night camp. During the day, with great regularity, they visit sunny plateaus, which are protected from the north wind by ledges, and camp there peacefully, soon enjoying themselves sprinting and teasing each other. From the valley one can frequently and easily observe the winter habits of these charming animals; for instance, from Lavin (Unterengadin) one can see flocks six, twenty, even forty-five-head strong, which in late fall gather from the rock desert of the Piz Linard, Schwarzhorn, Buin, etc. at the foot of Munt Chiapisun and spend there the grimmest season in relative comfort. All day long they appear always on their sunny camp and playground, and they move into the forest only towards evening.

After mating time, the chamois emaciate considerably, but not because of lack of food; this they find, with the exception of a short time during heavy snowfall, in all the mountains rather in abundance, though of less nutritious value. The short hay with dried-out stalks, from the windswept reservoirs and

Above the Gruenhornluecke (3,289 meters), a much-used passage from the Konkordia to the Fiescher glacier, the wind sweeps and drives the snow around the ridges and faces of the mountains. Wind is the great spoilsport of the alpine skier; it presses the loose powdery snow together into an unpleasant icedust (frozen snow) and transports it to those lee side slopes, where avalanches and snow slab dangers start.

59

southernly situated grass beds, has become hard, tough and straw-like and contrasts with the delicious fodder plants, the tender sprouts of the alpine elder, willow, raspberry bush during summer feeding. At the same time, in case of need, brushwood of pines, bark and moss have to help out, which they scrape out of the snow as reindeer do. Often they venture into the valley to springs on snow-free places; or they eat up the long sea-green beard moss which hangs down from the weather pines. When here and there a chamois entangles his horns in the branches, it remains suspended and starves. The same lichen which nourishes the animal was formerly used also by the hunter, who placed it as a stopper (plug, cork) for the powder in his rifle.

It is frequently observed that a fine instinct seems to teach the animals to prefer those forests, which are usually free of avalanches. Surely they cannot always be that lucky, and many a one must succumb to an avalanche. As soon as spring causes the snow cover of the higher mountains to thin, these alpine

Church-tower-deep crevasse of twin glacier at the ascent to Castor. This open crevasse shows impressively the danger which lurks for the alpine skier. The open crevasses which one can see are not as dangerous as the many still wider and deeper ones which are covered by snow bridges unable to withstand any loads.

Skiers in spring climb over hard frozen snow in the early morning towards the Giglistock (2,900 meters). Over the north ridge of the Sustenpeak (2,930 meters) the sun rises.
By the time the skiers have reached the summit, the sun has softened the snow so that a most pleasant ride downhill is anticipated.

animals rush back to their native homes and live half in the snow and half in the forests. To some extent, the chamois are the "reindeer of the Alps", as a poet might call them, and this not only because of their marvelous agility but also because of their contentedness, usefulness and resilient durability.

Where no other able alpine goat would dare to ascend to inaccessible grass beds on steepest mountain ledges, on footwide stone paths which wind themselves like a ribbon from summit to summit, there the chamois, as if destined by nature to exploit also this forlorn part of the plant offerings, bites off easily the scanty but hardy and nourishing plants of the Alps. By autumn they have become quite fat from it and weigh thirty, forty, (but not too often) fifty kilograms. One instance is known where a hunter of Glarn shot an animal which weighed sixty-two and a half kilograms, at Tschingeln. It was the huge and famous "Rufelibock", known by all hunters. This ram had for many years descended deeply into the valley and outsmarted the hunters, till finally the smart Blasi outwitted the clever Rufelibock. In 1870 a ram was shot on the Säntis, which, eviscerated, weighed forty-six kilograms. However, discovered skeletons lead occasionally to the conclusion that there existed in olden times far larger chamois than nowadays. Summer kids have in late fall grown to seven-and-a-half and even to ten kilograms.

Like all other ruminants, the chamois love salt to a high degree and therefore like to visit chalk rocks on which salty efflorescences can be found. After many hours of travel, the chamois come regularly to these "Sulzen" or "Glecken", especially if they are rich and situated close to water, which the chamois always seek out after licking the salt. The hunters themselves often take care of these "Sulzen" by sprinkling salt on them, but they do not like to shoot the chamois at this place because the animals may then avoid this territory for a long time.

As most animals of this kind, the chamois live together socially in groups of five, ten and up to twenty head. At one time flocks of sixty were not a rarity. They are lively, graceful and highly intelligent animals.

Each of their movements betrays an extraordinary muscular strength, agility, dexterity and gracefulness. This is especially the case when the animal is alerted or ready to jump. Otherwise they often stand around bow-legged and unattractive—as in confinement, when they drag their feet along; are *lau* ("timid"), as the hunters say; and have, even in the lowlands, a lazy and shuffling gait. Once startled, they change like lightning into a different nature and attain in their bold attitude something like genius. Their muscles become as tense and resilient as steel feathers, and, quick as the wind, they fly in magnificent leaps over canyons and ice. One must have seen it oneself in order to get an idea of the extraordinary volatility, of the astounding elasticity, of the incredible confidence in their movements and leaps. From one rock to another they jump over wide and deep abysses, keep their balance precariously, fling up their hind legs and

Panorama Following

View from an airplane over the highest peaks of the Bernese Alps. The camera is located in the northeast of the Finsteraarhorn at some 4,000 meters. The peaks of the Bernese Alps are not as high as those of the ice giants of Wallis, but their glacier formations are mightier. The great Aletschglacier, which flows to the valley between Gross-Wannenhorn (2) and Aletschhorn (7) is twenty-six kilometers long and the most powerful ice river of the Alps. Finsteraarhorn (14), the highest mountain in the Bernese Alps, had supposedly been climbed on August 14, 1812 from the Gemslücke (6) by the guides of the cartographer Johann Rudolf Meyer. This ascent has been doubted. On August 19, 1828 the guides of glacier scientist Franz Joseph Hugi reached the peak over today's normal route. Because of a foot injury Hugi had to stay back in the saddle below the peak. Now the saddle is named after Hugi (15).

The steep, gloomy northeast side of the Finsteraarhorn was the scene of a unique mountain climbing event in 1904. Twenty years before the general assault on the north face of the Alps, Gustav Hasler, with his guide Amatter, succeeded in the ascent of the very difficult ice-covered rocky face. How great this accomplishment was is proven by the fact that forty years later Hermann Waeffler and Otto Garecht succeeded in only the fourth ascent of it. On December 21 and 22, 1970 a guide from Wallenstadt, Paul Etter, with his companions Ueli Gantenbein, Andreas Scherrer, and Ernst Scheerer, overcame the face in a heavy gale and arctic cold. He compares the severities with those of the north face of the Matterhorn.

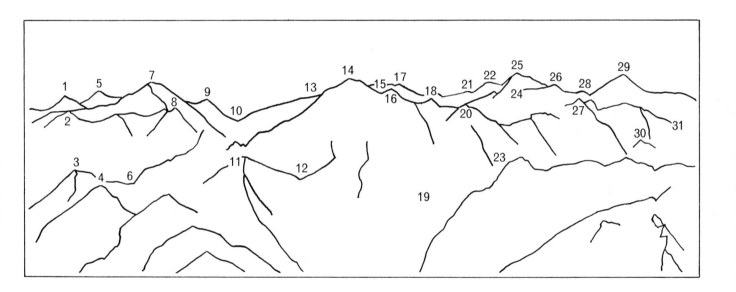

1. *Nesthorn 3,824 meters*
2. *Gross-Wannenhorn 3,905 meters*
3. *Finsteraar-Rothorn 3,530 meters*
4. *Oberaarhorn 3,638 meters*
5. *Bietschhorn 3,934 meters*
6. *Gemslücke 3,342 meters*
7. *Aletschhorn 4,195 meters*
8. *Fiescher Gabelhorn 3,875 meters*
9. *Sattelhorn 3,741 meters*
10. *Lötschenlücke 3,184 meters*
11. *Studerhorn 3,638 meters*

12. *Oberes Studerjoch 3,416 meters*
13. *Mittaghorn 3,897 meters*
14. *Finsteraarhorn 4,273 meters*
15. *Hugisattel 4,094 meters*
16. *Grosses Grünhorn 4,043 meters*
17. *Gletscherhorn 3,983 meters*
18. *Kleines Grünhorn 3,913 meters*
19. *Finsteraargletscher*
20. *Agassizhorn 3,953 meters*
21. *Kranzberg 3,737 meters*

22. *Rottalhorn 3,969 meters*
23. *Finsteraarjoch 3,290 meters*
24. *Hinter-Fiescherhorn 4,025 meters*
25. *Jungfrau 4,158 meters*
26. *Gross-Fiescherhorn 4,048 meters*
27. *Ochs 3,900 meters*
28. *Trugberg 3,932 meters*
29. *Mönch 4,099 meters*
30. *Pfaffenstöckli 3,114 meters*
31. *Berglihütte SAC 3,299 meters*

The fresh snow on the Fiescherglacier is one meter deep. The bad weather and the growing danger of avalanches have prompted a group of skiers to leave the Finsteraarhorn hut (3,050 meters) and to try a descent towards Fiesch.

safely reach a ledge not larger than a fist, at which they aim with a steady eye.

The extremely keen sense of smell of the chamois, their fine ear, their sense of direction developed to the highest potency, protects them from many dangers. When they camp in flocks, the animal that leads the herd—almost always a strong and older female—often takes over guard duty to a certain degree, although all other older animals also remain alert. While the younger ones graze, or play, or stab each other with their horns—as is the way of goats and deer—the female guard prefers to graze alone and at a distance. She looks about every other moment, stretches up, sniffs the air, walks to a ledge, and covers all sides. Suspecting danger, she whistles loudly, and all the others flee after her, never trotting but galloping.

This whistling of the chamois when in danger is often disputed; yet we can, from our own manifold experience, testify that it is heard almost every time when a flock of chamois is suddenly surprised. It is a husky, piercing, somewhat drawn-out tone, which probably passes through the front teeth, is sounded only once by the female guard and is not echoed by other chamois (as the marmots do).

The keenest sense organ of the chamois is without doubt that of their sense of smell; less sharp seems to be their eye, which often overlooks the barely hidden hunter. If he, on the other hand, is standing before the wind, the animals perceive him from an enormous distance—as well as from the side and from the bottom, because the air, warmed by the valley, rises up and carries to them the exudation of man. Immediately the senses of the chamois become extremely tense in order to find out the site of danger. Ear and eye compete with the sniffing nose. If they suspect the presence of a hunter without seeing him, the animal first noticing danger tramples the ground fiercely with its forefoot. Old chamois, out of anxiety, often behave wildly because they are not able to correct-

68

ly estimate either the closeness of the evil or its direction, and consequently lack a course of escape. Restlessly they run around or stand together, craning their necks to discover the hunter. As soon as this happens, they stop and examine him curiously for a moment. If he does not move, they too stand still; as soon as he stirs, they take a definite direction to a well-known and not far-off refuge. Very seldom does a fleeing and frightened animal, in leaping along rock faces, go so astray that it cannot move forward, and unable to turn, also cannot move backwards. Then it usually balances on the next ledge, lies on its belly close to the rock and endeavors to make the impossible possible. It leaps into the abyss and shatters. It is rare that a chamois "pretends", that it remains standing helplessly and hopelessly on an almost inaccessible ledge, as often do the bleating goats, who wait until the shepherd rescues them under risk of his own life. The chamois would rather plunge to its death. Nevertheless, this happens very rarely, since its judgment is above that of the goat. If the chamois comes to a narrow ledge, it remains standing before the abyss for a moment and then, often overcoming its fear of the man following it, turns swiftly as an arrow back the same way. Unless the hunter is by now well and securely positioned, it is high time for him to lie flat on the ground or to press himself closely against the rock, while the chamois flies by in sweeping leaps. If the animal, while being forced down on an almost vertical face of a rock, has no opportunity to reach a narrow ledge in order to soften a sharp fall, it lets itself down nevertheless with its head and neck pressed backwards and the weight of its body against its hind feet, which whir down sharply along the rock and so possibly delay the speed of the plunge. Indeed, the presence of mind of the animal is so enormous that, while letting itself down, if it notices a saving ledge, it paddles with body and feet to reach it and describes a curve while falling.

Snow, the ever present element in the Alps, is piled up and molded by the wind into art forms.

It is rare to see an old ram with a herd. They live very secluded and reach an age of thirty years, when their heads become almost totally gray. The younger animals separate from the herd only in November, during breeding time. Violent struggles between rams occur during this time, which lasts to the middle of January, and often end badly. Either one ram is pushed over the rocks or a stronger one, who beats fiercely with his horns, or one fatally wounds another or pursues it for hours. The female goat follows the victor willingly and lives alone with him until the onset of deep winter, when both return to their own herds. The pregnant female carries for twenty weeks and bears one or two young at the end of April or the end of May, usually under a dry and hidden overhang. She suckles her young for six months yet one often sees one- and two-year-olds drinking from their mother's breast. The ram is not concerned about his children. The young do not become reproductive and acquire horns until their third year. During their first year they bleat like goats. When they are only hours old, their mother licks them clean, and they follow her everywhere. When they are twelve hours old, man is no longer able to overtake them.

In the stomach of the chamois, especially in that of older rams, and several others of the same species, one often finds the so-called "chamois-bullet", or the *deutsche Bezoarstein*. These are hazelnut- to chicken-egg-sized balls of dark vegetable fiber and bast cells coated with a shining and aromatic substance. They are probably the residue of undigested vegetable fibers, which forms together with the resinous components of devoured buds and shrubs, as well as with the animal gelatine and licked-off hairs.

Through the peristaltic movement of the stomach, a ball gradually builds up from new accumulation of undigestible matter. Entire books have been written about the healing power of these chamois balls; they are supposed to cure all kinds of evil, even make soldiers bullet proof, and have been purchased with a Louisdor and more.

Up there on the highest rocky slopes of the Alps, where trees or brush no longer grow, where no cattle and few goats or sheep venture to anymore—there, even on small rock islands in the midst of huge glaciers, is the home of the

The morning sun reddens the Matterhorn (4,477 meters), the most powerful rock pyramid of the Alps. The view from Festigglacier at the dome shows the north and east face of the mountain, which is separated by the Hoernli ridge, the route of the first mountaineers. On July 14, 1865 the Englishmen Edward Whymper, Charles Hudson, D. R. Hadow, and Francis Douglas, together with guides Michel Auguste Croz and Peter Taugwalter and son, conquered the mountain for the first time. One of the most memorable events in the history of alpine mountain climbing had taken place. This triumph was darkened by a catastrophe: Croz, Hudson, Hadow, and Douglas plunged from the shoulder over the north side to their death.

A rope team climbs the Hoernli ridge of the Matterhorn towards the Solvay hut. The Matterhorn is a pure rock mountain, and whoever climbs over the Hoernli ridge never sets foot on a glacier. The ascent of the Hoernli ridge is technically easy and is simplified by ropes anchored at the upper sections. Nevertheless, the Matterhorn remains a dangerous peak, notorious for sudden changes in weather.

marmot. Equipped for a partly underground existence, it is satisfied with the small field of nutriment in the vicinity of its habitat. It knows how to defend itself vigorously against any intruder by biting and scratching. On the other hand, during the cold season when the animal struggles to find the means to sustain its life, nature protects it by putting it into a long lethargic sleep, without which the animal would surely succumb to hunger and the enemies it encounters in its wanderings.

Summer life is pleasant for the animals. At dawn the old ones appear first at the exit of their tunnel, peek out carefully, search, listen, examine the surroundings for anything strange and slowly dare to come out; then they walk a few steps

71

uphill, perform a few somersaults, and finally have breakfast. With enormous speed they graze bare even the shortest grass while continuously being on the look-out. Apparently they search especially for the blossoms of small alpine plants, because these have quickly disappeared in a rather wide circle after the marmots have grazed in a certain place. Soon after their parents, the young emerge from their burrow without much ado and begin to graze too. Normally, as soon as they are filled they lie down on a certain spot, preferably a comfortable stone in the sun.

This traditional place of rest must not be far away from the entrance of their burrow and is always noticeable, as is the thousand-times-treaded path to it, because both literally look polished. Time is passed now with resting and playing. Every other moment they sit up on their hind legs, look around, clean, scratch and comb themselves, play and romp with each other; young ones have been seen trying to stand upright on their hind legs and walk a few steps. In the

Climber at the rise of the Furggen ridge. The Furggen ridge is the steepest and most difficult ridge on the Matterhorn. It forms the dividing line between the east and south face of the mountain and is simultaneously the border line between Switzerland and Italy. In 1911 Mario Piacenza, with Jean Joseph Carrel and Joseph Gaspard, made the first successful ascent to the peak. In the normal ascent today, the traversing to the brittle south face is limited to cases of the utmost necessity. It was opened in 1930 by Enzo Benedetti, Luigi Carrel, and Maurice Bich.

Sunrise on the Matterhorn. The wrought-iron cross stands on the Italian peak. One arm points to Valtournanche and carries the inscription VALLISTORNENCIS; *the other, in the direction of Zermatt, carries the inscription* PRATUMBORNUM— *"Meadow surrounded by boundary stones"—a very old designation for Zermatt.*

meantime, old animals watch over the territory. At any suspicious sign, be it a bird of prey, a fox, a man, and even if it is hours away, the first marmot to become aware of it whistles in short pauses through its teeth, announcing it far and wide over the area. The tone of the whistle, which is heard daily numberless times in the Alps, is deep rather than high, often in long, eerie sounds, yet harsh and piercing. According to exact observations, only those animals which have themselves seen the cause of danger repeat the whistling. If only the animal that gave the signal has noticed the danger and hurried to the tunnel, all others will pursue without whistling. The signaling animal, however, flees only when danger is near. As long as man or beast of prey remain still at a distance, the alarm whistle is incessantly repeated. All marmots of the entire vast mountain range look constantly for the enemy, and from all planks and slopes sounds the signal that they are aware of him there, too. If the enemy is hiding behind a rock and remains still, the signals stop. But the animals are on their guard, and they whistle again as soon as the enemy reappears. If, however, he nears or makes any drastic or conspicuous gestures, the closest animals disappear quickly into the burrow.

Those who flee without whistling and disappear without having seen the enemy reappear sooner than the others. It has not been proven that the marmots really post guards, as do the chamois; it is in fact denied by all hunters. The smallness and coloring of the animals protect them from danger; but even more effective is their magnificently sharp and shining eye, that perceives man at a distance at which even man's best telescope cannot see the animal. During raw weather the marmots do not leave their burrow for days, not even at night. After the sun has set, all playgrounds and grazing grounds are empty, often in fall soon after midday. If, during a day in this season, they have been alerted by a whistle, they hardly leave the burrow anymore that same day.

The main tunnel of their winter quarters is seldom shorter than one to two

73

meters, estimated from the entrance, but is believed often to measure eight or ten meters. Towards the end, it usually slopes upward and leads into an elongated or rounded cave or chamber, one to two meters in diameter, 90 to 120 centimeters deep beneath the sod; the ground is covered with short, soft, dry, usually reddish-brown hay that will be partially replaced with fresh hay towards fall. By August, in fine weather, the smart marmot has already busily begun to bite off grass and shrubs and, after these have dried, to carry them in its muzzle into the burrow. A fable-like story by Plynius, handed down to this day, says that the alp mice (marmots) bring the fodder into the caves in such a way that one of them lies on his back and is loaded with hay held fast to his body, while another marmot seizes it by the tail with his teeth and pulls it into the cave. That is why the back of the marmot looks so abraded. The origin of this fable can be easily understood by noticing the sticky hair found at each tunnel entrance.

The summer habitat never contains hay, while the winter habitat often contains so much that one man would hardly be able to carry it away. It is still not determined whether the animals, in certain cases, use the hay covering for fodder also. Schinz and Roemer surmise with good reason that this may happen when sunny spring days cause an early awakening and then, through a sudden return of raw winter weather, the aroused animals cannot find food. Marmots held in captivity and aroused from their winter sleep eat with a hearty appetite. If a hunter uncovers a kettle hole, he finds there an entire family—often ten to fifteen marmots—lying together in deathlike stiffness. The temperature of the cave is 10 or 11 degrees centigrade. The animals are rolled together with their noses touching their tails and their hind legs close to the sides of their heads. In this position, "lethargy conservatrice", Mother Nature in a wondrous way protects her children, which during six to eight months of the long alpine winter would certainly perish without this saving plant-like sleep. During this time they do not take any nourishment. Since breathing stops almost entirely, there is no need of food. With food denied them, the lungs lack the necessary supplies for fuel and warmth, the organism cools off, and dormancy is complete. The marmot probably enters at first into a longer ordinary sleep. With the low temperature of the kettle hole and the long fast, together with the absolute motionlessness, it then appears to enter the lethargic winter sleep from which, as a rule, it does not awaken before April.

In case unearthings disturb the marmots in their winter habitat before they have fallen into deep sleep, they skillfully and happily dig themselves further into the mountain and so protect themselves from man.

Leslie Stephen (1832–1904) An ex-clergyman and professor of mathematics, Sir Leslie Stephen belonged to that small circle of adventurous Englishmen who during the "Golden Age" of alpinism climbed most of the mountains of 4,000 meters or higher in the Alps. He was an excellent mountaineer and a brilliant author with a good sense of humor. His stories, published under the title The Playground of Europe *make him one of the great writers of alpinism. In "The Rothhorn" Stephen describes the first assault of the Zinalrothorn via the northern ridge.*

6 LESLIE STEPHEN

The Rothhorn

The little village of Zinal lies, as I need hardly inform my readers, deep in the recesses of the Pennine chain. Some time in the Middle Ages (I speak on the indisputable authority of Murray) the inhabitants of the surrounding valleys were converted to Christianity by the efforts of a bishop of Sion. From that time till the year 1864 I know little of its history, with the exception of two facts—one, that till lately the natives used holes in their tables as a substitute for plates, each member of the family depositing promiscuously his share of the family meals in his own particular cavity; the other, that a German traveller was murdered between Zinal and Evolena in 1863. This information, however, meagre as it is, illustrates the singular retirement from the world of these exquisite valleys. The great road of the Simplon has for years carried crowds of travellers past the opening of their gorges. Before its construction, Rousseau and Goethe had celebrated the charms of the main valley. During the last twenty years Zermatt has been the centre of attraction for thousands of tourists. And yet, so feeble is the curiosity of mankind, and so sheeplike are the habits of the ordinary traveller, that these remote fastnesses still retain much of their primitive seclusion. Evolena, Zinal, and the head of the Turtman Thal, are still visited only by a few enthusiasts. Even the Saas valley, easily accessible as it is, and leading to one of the most justly celebrated of Alpine passes, attracts scarcely one in a hundred of the many visitors to the twin valley of Zermatt. And yet those who have climbed the slopes behind the village and seen the huge curtain of ice let down from the summits of the mighty range between the Dom and Monte Rosa, cutting off half the horizon as with a more than gigantic screen, will admit that its beauties are almost unique in the Alps. Mr. Wills did justice to them long ago; but, in spite of all that can be said, the tourist stream flows in its old channels and leaves on either side regions of enchanting beauty, but almost as little visited as the remote valleys of Norway. I remember a striking scene near Grüben, in the Turtman

75

The Mischabel group rises above the ridge of the Bishorn. In the middle of the picture is the Dom (4,545 meters), the highest mountain peak of the Alps situated entirely in Switzerland. Its ascent from Randa via the Festi ridge is long but technically easy. The Täschhorn to the right of the Dom is a little lower (4,490 meters) and not easy to climb. Next to the Täschhorn is the wide top of the Alpenhubel. To the left of the Dom are the Lenzspitze and the Nadelhorn.

Thal, which curiously exemplified this fact. We were in a little glade surrounded by pine forest, and with the Alpine rose clustering in full bloom round the scattered boulders. Above us rose the Weisshorn in one of the most sublime aspects of that almost faultless mountain. The Turtman glacier, broad and white with deep regular crevasses, formed a noble approach, like the staircase of some superb palace. Above this rose the huge mass of the mountain, firm and solid as though its architect had wished to eclipse the Pyramids. And, higher still, its lofty crest, jagged and apparently swaying from side to side seemed to be tossed into the blue atmosphere far above the reach of mortal man. Nowhere have I seen a more delicate combination of mountain massiveness, with soaring and delicately carved pinnacles pushed to the verge of extravagance. Yet few people know this side of a peak, which every one has admired from the Riffel. The only persons who shared our view, though they could hardly share our wonder, were a little group of peasants standing round a small châlet. A herd of cows had been collected, and a priest in tattered garments was sprinkling them with holy water. They received us much as we might have been received in the least frequented of European districts, and it was hard to remember that we were within a short walk of the main post route and Mr. Cook's tourists. We seemed to have stepped into the Middle Ages, though I fancied that some shade of annoyance showed itself on the faces of the party, as of men surprised in a rather superstitious observance. Perhaps they had a dim impression that we might be smiling in our sleeves, and knew that beyond their mountain wall were sometimes to be seen daring sceptics, who doubted the efficacy of holy water as a remedy for rinderpest. We of course expressed no opinion upon the subject, and passed on with a friendly greeting, reflecting how a trifling inequality in the earth's surface may be the means of preserving the relics of extinct modes of thought. But, for that matter, a London lane or an old college wall may be as effectual a prophylactic: even a properly cut coat is powerful in repelling contagion.

76

Leaving such meditations, I may remark that Swiss enterprise has begun to penetrate these retired valleys. It is a mystery, of difficult solution, how the spiders which live in certain retired and, as we would think, flyless corners of ancient libraries, preserve their existence; but it is still harder to discover how innkeepers in these rarely trodden valleys derive sufficient supplies from the mere waifs and strays that are thrown, as it were, from the main body of tourists. However that may be, a certain M. Epinay maintains a hospitable inn at Zinal, which has since been much enlarged; and the arrival of Grove, Macdonald, and myself, with our guides Melchior and Jacob Anderegg, in August 1864, rather more than doubled the resident population. M. Epinay's inn, I may remark, is worthy of the highest praise. It is true that the accommodation was then limited. Macdonald and Grove had to sleep in two cupboards opening out of the coffee-room, whilst I occupied a bed, which was the most conspicuous object of furniture in the coffee-room itself. The only complaint I could find with it was that whenever I sat up suddenly I brought my head into violent contact with the ceiling. This peculiarity was owing to a fourth bed, which generally lurked beneath the legs of my rather lofty couch, but could be drawn out on due occasion. The merits of the establishment in other respects were manifold. Above all, M. Epinay is an excellent cook, and provided us daily with dinners which—I almost shrink from saying it—were decidedly superior to those of my excellent friend M. Seiler, at Zermatt. Inns, however, change almost as rapidly as dynasties, and I do not extend these remarks to the present day. Finally, the room boasted of one of the few decent sofas in Switzerland. It is true that it was only four feet long, and terminated by two lofty barriers; but it was soft, and had cushions—an unprecedented luxury, so far as my alpine knowledge extends. The minute criticism of M. Epinay's establishment is due to the fact that we spent there three days of enforced idleness.

Nothing is more delightful than fine weather in the Alps; but, as a general rule, the next thing to it is bad weather in the Alps. There is scarcely a day in summer when a man in ordinary health need be confined to the house; and even in the dreariest state of the atmosphere, when the view is limited to a few yards

At the lower end of the Festi glacier is the Dom shelter of the Uto Section of SAC. It is 2,928 meters high and was built by the well-known shelter architect Jakob Eschenmoser. During the peak season (July–August) it is run by inn-keeper Brantschen from Randa.

When climbing from the Dom shelter across the Festi glacier to the Festi ridge, the mountaineer can enjoy a fabulous view by looking back over his shoulder. Above the fog-covered Matter valley the Weisshorn rises in the first sunlight. To the left the Zinalrothorn and the Obergabelhorn.

by driving mists on some lofty pasturage, there are infinite beauties of detail to be discovered by persons of humble minds. Indeed, on looking back to days spent in the mountains, I sometimes think that the most enjoyable have been, not those of unbroken sunshine, but those on which one was forcibly confined to admiring some little vignette of scenery strangely transfigured by the background of changing cloud. The huge boulder under which you take refuge, the angry glacier torrent dashing out of obscurity and disappearing in a few yards, and the cliff whose summit and base are equally concealed by the clouds, gain wonderfully in dignity and mystery. Yet I must confess that when one is suffering from an acute attack of the climbing fever, and panting for an opportunity which will not come, the patience is tried for the moment, even though striking fragments of scenery may be accumulating in the memory.

A persistent screen of stormy cloud drove up the valley, and clung stubbornly to the higher peaks. We lounged lazily in the wooded gallery, smoking our pipes and contemplating the principal street of the village. Once, as I sat there peacefully, a little pack of mountain stoats dashed in full cry across the village street; the object of chase was invisible; one might easily fancy that some quaint mountain goblin was the master of the hounds; if so, he did not reveal himself to the unworthy eyes of one of those tourists who are frightening him and his like from their native haunts. Once or twice an alarm of natives was raised; and we argued long whether they were inhabitants, or merely visitors from the neighbouring Alps come to see life in Zinal. I incline to the latter hypothesis, being led thereto from a consideration of the following circumstances:—One of our desperate efforts at amusement was playing cricket in the high street, with a rail for a bat, and a small granite boulder for a ball. My first performance was a brilliant hit to leg (the only one I ever made in my life) off Macdonald's bowling. To my horror I sent the ball clean through the western window of the chapel, which

78

looks upon the *grande place* of the village—the scene of our match. As no one ever could be found to receive damages, I doubt much whether there are any permanent inhabitants. Tired of cricket, I learnt the visitors' book by heart; I studied earnestly the remarks of a deaf and dumb gentleman, who, for some mysterious reason, has selected this book as the chief medium of communication with the outer world. I made, I fear, rather ill-tempered annotations on some of my predecessors' remarks. I even turned a table of heights expressed in mètres into feet, and have thereby contributed richly to the fund of amusement provided for scientific visitors who may have a taste for correcting arithmetical blunders. On Sunday the weather was improving, and after breakfast we lounged up the Diablons—an easy walk, if taken from the right direction. The view met with our decided disapproval—principally, perhaps, because we did not see it, and partly because we had taken no provisions; a thunderstorm drenched us during our descent, and I began to think the weather hopeless. The same evening, as I was reclining on the sofa, in the graceful attitude of a V, whose extremities were represented by my head and feet, and whose apex was plunged in the before-mentioned cushions, the sanguine Macdonald said that the weather was clearing up. My reply was expressive of that utter disbelief with which a passenger in a Channel steamboat resents the steward's assurance that Calais is in sight. Next morning, however, at 1.50 A.M., I found myself actually crossing the meadows which form the upper level of the Zinal valley. It was a cloudless night, except that a slight haze obscured the distant Oberland ridges. But for the disheartening influence of a prolonged sojourn in Zinal, I might have been sanguine. As it was, I walked in that temper of gloomy disgust which I find to be a frequent concomitant of early rising. Another accident soon happened to damp our spirits. Macdonald was forced to give in to a sharp attack of illness, which totally incapacitated him for a difficult expedition. We parted with him with great regret, and proceeded gloomily on our way. Poor Macdonald spent the day dismally enough, I fear, in the little inn, in the company of M. Epinay and certain German tourists.

We followed the usual track for the Trift pass as far as the top of the great icefall of the Durand glacier. Here we turned sharply to the left, and crossed the wilderness of decaying rock at the foot of Lo Besso. It is a strangely wild scene. The buttresslike mass of Lo Besso cut off our view of the lower country. Our path led across a mass of huge loose rocks, which I can only compare to a continuous series of the singular monuments known as rocking-stones. For a second or two you balanced yourself on a mass as big as a cottage, and balanced not only yourself but the mass on which you stood. As it canted slowly over, you made a convulsive spring, and lighted upon another rock in an equally unstable position. If you were lucky you recovered yourself by a sudden jerk, and prepared for the next leap. If unlucky, you landed with your knees, nose, and other

At an altitude of 3,256 meters on the Col de Tracuit, there is the Tracuit shelter of the Chaussy section of the SAC. The location of the shelter is unique. It is close to a majestic circle of peaks and glaciers. In the clouds of a summer evening such mighty peaks as that of the Zinalrothorn, the Obergabelhorn, the Dent Blanche, the Matterhorn, and the Dent d'Hérens appear. Climbing the Bishorn from the Tracuit shelter is one of the simplest ascents of a 4,000-meter-high mountain in the Alps. Traversing the Weisshorn ridge is part of one of the classical alpine tours.

The arctic world on the Dom (4,545 meters). Even in the middle of summer there can be cold winds blowing across the wide snow fields of the upper Hohberg glacier. The normal route to the roof of Switzerland is not very difficult, but rather strenuous because of the significant difference in altitude.

parts of your person in contact with various lumps of rock, and got up into an erect posture by another series of gymnastic contortions. In fact, my attitudes, at least, were as unlike as possible to that of Mercury—

New lighted on a heaven-kissing hill.

They were more like Mercury shot out of a cart on to a heap of rubbish. An hour or so of this work brought us to a smooth patch of rocks, from which we obtained our first view of the Rothhorn, hitherto shut out by a secondary spur of the Besso. And here, at 5.50 A.M., we halted for breakfast. 'How beautiful those clouds are!' was Grove's enthusiastic remark as we sat down to our frozen meal. The rest of the party gave a very qualified response to his admiration of a phenomenon beautiful in itself, but ominous of bad weather. For my part, I never profess to be in a good temper at six o'clock in the morning. Christian morality appears to me to become binding every morning at breakfast-time, that is, about 9.30 A.M. Macdonald's departure had annoyed me. A more selfish dislike to the stones over which we had been stumbling had put me out still further. The bitterest drop in my cup was the state of the weather. The sky overhead, indeed, was still cloudless; but just before the Besso eclipsed the Oberland ridges, an offensive mist had blotted out their serrated outline. I did not like the way in which the stars winked at us just before their disappearance in the sunlight. But worst of all was a heavy mass of cloud which clung to the ridge between the Dent Blanche and the Gabelhorn, and seemed to be crossing the Col de Zinal, under the influence of a strong south wind. The clouds, to which Grove unfeelingly alluded, were a detachment, rising like steam from a cauldron above this lower mass. They seemed to gather to leeward of the vast cliffs of the Dent Blanche, and streamed out from their shelter into the current of the gale which evidently raged above our heads. At this moment they were tinged with every

82

shade of colour that an alpine sunrise can supply. I have heard such clouds described as 'mashed rainbow'; and whatever the nature of the culinary process, their glorious beauty is undeniable. But for the time the ambition of climbing the Rothhorn had quenched all aesthetic influences, and a sulky growl was the only homage I could pay them.

Yet one more vexatious element was here intruded into our lot. We were in full view of the Rothhorn, to which we had previously given a careful examination from the foot of the Trift-Joch. As this is the most favourable moment for explaining our geography, I will observe that we were now within the hollow embraced by the spur which terminates in the great promontory of Lo Besso. This spur has its origin in the main ridge which runs from the Rothhorn towards the Weisshorn, the point of articulation being immediately under the final cliffs of the Rothhorn. It divides the Moming glacier from the upper snows of the Durand glacier. The mighty 'cirque' inclosed by the mountain wall—studded in

Englishman J. Llewelyn Davies, who first climbed the Dom, soon complained about the absence of comfortable seats on the peak of the Dom. "There are no boulders and the wind blows unobstructed across the snowy platform. One has to enjoy the great view while standing. What a view!" With chattering teeth Taugwald insisted that it was much more grandiose than that from the even higher Monte Rosa. We can look from the peak of the Dom to the neighboring Weisshorn.

succession by the peaks of the Besso, the Rothhorn, the Gabelhörner, the Dent Blanche, and the Grand Cornier—is one of the very noblest in the Alps. From the point we had now reached it appeared to form a complete amphitheatre, the narrow gorge through which the Durand glacier emerges into the Einfischthal being invisible. Our plan of operations was to climb the spur (of which I have already spoken) about half-way between Lo Besso and the Rothhorn, and thence to follow it up to the top of the mountain. The difficulty, as we had early foreseen, would begin just after the place where the spur blended with the northern ridge of the Rothhorn. We had already examined with our telescopes the narrow and broken arête which led upwards from this point to the summit. Its scarped and perpendicular sides, and the rocky teeth which struck up from its back, were sufficiently threatening. Melchior had, notwithstanding, spoken with unusual confidence of our chance. But at this moment the weakest point in his character developed itself. He began to take a gloomy view of his prospects, and to confide his opinion to Jacob Anderegg in what he fondly imagined to be unintelligible patois. I understood him only too well. 'Jacob,' he said, 'we shall get up to that rock, and then—' an ominous shake of the head supplied the remainder of the sentence. It was therefore in sulky silence that, after half an hour's halt, I crossed the snow-field, reached the top of the spur at 7.55 A.M., and thence ascended the arête to within a short distance of the anticipated difficulty. Our progress was tolerably rapid, being only delayed by the necessity of cutting some half-dozen steps. We were at a great height, and the eye plunged into the Zinal valley on one side, and to the little inn upon the Riffel on the other, whilst on looking round it commanded the glacier basin from which we had just ascended. Close beneath us, to the north, was the col by which Messrs. Moore and Whymper had passed from the Moming to the Schallenberg glacier. It was now 9 A.M. We cowered under the rocky parapet which here strikes up through the snow like a fin from a fish's back, and guarded us from the assaults of a fierce southern gale. All along the arête to this point I had distinctly felt a keen icy blast penetrate my coat as though it had been made of gossamer, pierce my skin, whistle merrily through my ribs, and, after chilling the internal organs, pass out

In the early morning light the Monte Rosa massif with its highest peak, the Dufour-spitze (4,634 meters), appears above the twin glacier. The peak which bears its name in honor of the great cartographer and general Henri Dufour is the highest one in Switzerland. From the Monte Rosa shelter it can even be reached on skis across the flat Monte Rosa glacier. In the east it falls off towards the Italian Macugnaga as the highest ice wall of the Alps.

at the other side with unabated vigour. My hands were numb, my nose was doubtless purple, and my teeth played involuntary airs, like the bones of a negro minstrel. Grove seemed to me to be more cheerful than circumstances justified. By way, therefore, of reducing his spirits nearer to freezing-point—or let me hope, in the more laudable desire of breaking his too probable disappointment —I invented for his benefit a depressing prophecy supposed to have been just uttered by Melchior; and, if faces can speak without words, my gloomy prediction was not entirely without justification.

We were on a ledge of snow which formed a kind of lean-to against the highest crest of precipitous rock. A little further on the arête made a slight elbow, beyond which we could see nothing. If the snowy shelf continued beyond the elbow, all might yet be well. If not, we should have to trust ourselves to the tender mercies of the seamed and distorted rocks. A very few paces settled the question. The snow thinned out. We turned to examine the singular ridge along which the only practicable path must lie. From its formation it was impossible to see more than a very short way ahead. So steep were the precipices on each side that to our imaginations it had all the effect of a thin wall, bending in its gradual decay first towards one and then towards the other valley. The steep faces of rock thus appeared to overhang the Schallenberg and Zinal glaciers alternately. The same process of decay had gradually carved the parapet which surmounted it into fantastic pinnacles, and occasionally scored deep channels in its sides. It was covered with the rocky fragments rent off by the frost, and now lying in treacherous repose, frequently masked by cushions of fresh-fallen snow. The cliffs were, at times, as smooth as if they had been literally cut out by the sweep of a gigantic knife. But the smooth faces were separated by deep gullies, down which the artillery of falling stones was evidently accustomed to play. I fear that I can very imperfectly describe the incidents of our assault upon this formidable

Among the many Breithorns in Switzerland the Wallis Breithorn is the highest. From the south it could possibly be the 4,000-meter-high mountain of the Alps which is easiest to climb, while in the north it breaks off into tall walls towards the Gorner glacier. The ascent up the ice wall, interspersed with rocks, belongs to the great tours in the Zermatt area. Here mountain guides Paul Etter and René Arnold are climbing towards the peak on the Welzenbach trail.

Climbing the Mittellegi ridge on the Eiger is made easier because of the shelter built by the Grindelwald mountain guide association. The wooden hut, covered with shingles, is situated on the lower part of the ridge. The mountaineer uses the precious fuel sparingly and is his own chef in the kitchen.

fortress. Melchior led us with unfaltering skill—his spirits, as usual, rising in proportion to the difficulty, when the die had once been cast. Three principal pinnacles rose in front of us, each of which it was necessary to turn or to surmount. The first of these was steepest upon the Zinal side. Two deep gullies on the Zermatt side started from points in the ridge immediately in front and in rear of the obstacle, and converged at some distance beneath. The pinnacle itself was thus shaped like a tooth protruding from a jaw and exposed down to the sockets, and the two gullies afforded means for circumventing it. We carefully descended by one of these for some distance, considerably inconvenienced by the snow which lodged in the deeply-cut channels, and concealed the loose stones. With every care it was impossible not occasionally to start crumbling masses of rock. The most ticklish part of the operation was in crossing to the other gully; a sheet of hard ice some two or three inches thick covered the steeply-inclined slabs. It was impossible to cut steps in it deep enough to afford secure foothold. The few knobs of projecting stone seemed all to be too loose either for hand or foot. We crept along in as gingerly a fashion as might be, endeavouring to distribute our weight over the maximum number of insecure supports until one of the party had got sounder footing. A severe piece of chimneysweep practice then landed us once more upon the razor edge of the arête. The second pinnacle demanded different tactics. On the Zermatt side it was impractically steep, whilst on the other it fell away in one of the smooth sheets of rock already mentioned. The rock, however, was here seamed by deep fissures approximately horizontal. It was possible to insert toes or fingers into these, so as to present to telescopic vision (if anyone had been watching our ascent) much the appearance of a fly on a pane of glass. Or, to make another comparison, our method of progression was not unlike that of the caterpillars, who may be observed first doubled up into a loop and then stretched out at full

The highest peak in Switzerland, the 4,634-meter Dufour, breaks off to a steep slope in the east. The ascent to the Dufour peak up the 2,-000-meter-high Monte Rosa east wall is long, strenuous, and often dangerous. Mountain guide Romedi Spada is climbing on the rocks of the Dufour peak.

length. When two crevices approximated, we should be in danger of treading on our own fingers, and the next moment we should be extended as though on the rack, clutching one crack with the last joints of our fingers, and feeling for another with the extreme points of our toes. The hold was generally firm when the fissures were not filled with ice, and we gradually succeeded in outflanking the second hostile position. The third, which now rose within a few yards, was of far more threatening appearance than its predecessors. After a brief inspection, we advanced along the ridge to its base. In doing so we had to perform a manoeuvre which, though not very difficult, I never remember to have previously tried. One of the plates to Berlepsch's description of the Alps represents a mountain-top, with the national flag of Switzerland waving from the summit and a group of enthusiastic mountaineers swarming round it. One of them approaches, astride of a sharp ridge, with one leg hanging over each precipice. Our position was similar, except that the ridge by which we approached consisted of rock instead of snow. The attitude adopted had the merit of safety, but was deficient in comfort. The rock was so smooth, and its edge so sharp, that as I crept along it, supported entirely on my hands, I was in momentary fear that a slip might send one-half of me to the Durand and the other to the Schallenberg glacier. It was, however, pleasing to find a genuine example of the arête in its normal state—so often described in books, and so seldom found in real life. We landed on a small platform at the other end of our razor of *Al Sirat,* hoping for the paradise of a new mountain summit as our reward; but as we looked upwards at the last of the three pinnacles, I felt doubtful of the result.

The rock above us was, if I am not mistaken, the one which, by its sharp inclination to the east, gives to the Rothhorn, from some points of view, the appearance of actually curling over in that direction, like the crest of a sea-wave on the point of breaking. To creep along the eastern face was totally impossible. The western slopes, though not equally steep, were still frightfully precipitous, and presented scarcely a ledge whereby to cling to their slippery surface. In front of us the rocks rose steeply in a very narrow crest, rounded and smooth at the top, and with all foothold, if foothold there were, completely concealed by a layer of fresh snow. After a glance at this somewhat unpromising path, Melchior examined for a moment the western cliff. The difficulties there seeming even greater, he immediately proceeded to the direct assault. In a few minutes I was scrambling desperately upwards, forgetting in a moment the promptings of the self-esteem which would generally induce me to refuse assistance and to preserve a workmanlike attitude. So steeply did the precipice sink on our left hand, that along the whole of this part of the shelf the glacier at a vast distance below, formed the immediate background to a sloping rocky ledge, some foot or two in width, and covered by slippery snow. In a few paces I found myself fumbling vaguely with my fingers at imaginary excrescences, my feet resting upon rotten projections of crumbling stone, whilst a large pointed slab of rock pressed

88

The Eiger (3,970 meters) with its north wall as seen from an airplane. Above it the Finsteraarhorn, the Fiescherhörner, the Grünhorn, and the Wannenhorn. During the last thirty years climbing of the dark 1700-meter-high wall has contributed a great deal to giving alpinism the reputation of being very daring, even suicidal. Like no other great wall in the Alps the Eiger wall with its danger of falling rocks is ideal for climbing. At the foot of the Eiger is a great tourist attraction, the Small Scheidegg, from which a great number of tourists and reporters can observe what is happening on the wall. After several attempts and fatal accidents, the alpinists Anderl Heckmair, Ludwig Vörg, Fritz Kasparek, and Heinrich Harrer were the first to climb it on July 21–23, 1938.

against my stomach, and threatened to force my centre of gravity backwards beyond the point of support. My chief reliance was upon the rope; and with a graceful flounder I was presently landed in safety upon a comparatively sound ledge. Looking backwards, I was gratified by a picture which has since remained fixed in my imagination. Some feet down the steep ridge was Grove, in one of those picturesque attitudes which a man involuntarily adopts when the various points to which he trusts his weight have been distributed without the least regard to the exigencies of the human figure, when they are of a slippery and crumbling nature, and when the violent downward strain of the rope behind him is only just counterbalanced by the upward strain of the rope in front. Below Grove appeared the head, shoulders, and arms of Jacob. His fingers were exploring the rock in search of infinitesimal crannies, and his face presented the expression of modified good humour, which in him supplies the place of extreme discontent in other guides. Jacob's head and shoulders were relieved against the snows of the Schallenberg glacier many hundred feet below. Our view of continuous rock was thus limited to a few yards of narrow ridge, tilted up at a steep angle apparently in mid air; and Jacob resembled a man in the act of clambering into a balloon far above the earth. I had but little time for contemplation before turning again to our fierce strife with the various impediments to our march. Suddenly Melchior, who had left the highest ridge to follow a shelf of rock on the right, turned to me with the words, 'In half an hour we shall be on the top.' My first impulse was to express an utter scepticism. My perturbed imagination was unable to realise the fact that we should ever get off the arête any more. We seemed to be condemned to a fate which Dante might have reserved for faithless guides—to be everlastingly climbing a hopeless arête, in a high wind, and never getting any nearer the summit. Turning an angle of the rock, I saw that he had spoken the truth, and for the first time that day it occurred to me that life was not altogether a mistake. We had reached the top of what I have called the third pinnacle, and with it our difficulties were over. In the words of the poet, modified to the necessary extent—

> He that with toil of heart and knees and hands
> Up the long ridge to the far height hath won
> His path upwards, and prevailed,
> Shall find the toppling crags of the Rothhorn scaled—

are close to what, by a somewhat forced metaphor, we may call 'a shining tableland.' It is not a particularly level nor a very extensive tableland; but, compared with the ridges up which we had been forcing our precarious way, it was luxurious in the extreme. 'Twas not so wide as Piccadilly nor so level as the Bedford river, but 'twould serve; I might almost add, if the metaphor were not somewhat strained, that it made 'worm's meat' of the Rothhorn. At any rate it was sound under-foot, and broad enough for practical purposes; and within less than Melchior's half-hour, viz. 11:15 A.M., we reached—I had almost said the top; but the Rothhorn has no top. It has a place where a top manifestly ought to have been, but the work had been left unfinished. It ended in a flat circular area a few feet broad, as though it had been a perfect cone, with the apex cleanly struck off. Melchior and Jacob set to work at once to remedy this deficiency of nature, whilst Grove and I cowered down in a little hole cut out of the last rocks, which sheltered us from the bitter wind. Here, in good temper with each other and our guides, and everything but Macdonald's absence, we sat down for some twenty minutes, with muscles still quivering from the strain.

No doubt some enthusiast will ask me about the view. I have several times been asked what the Matterhorn looked like; and I wish I could give an answer. But I will make a clean breast of it, and confess that I only remember two things: one, that we saw the Riffelberg, looking like a flat green carpet; the other, that the gigantic mass of the Weisshorn seemed to frown right above our heads, and shut out a large segment from the view. Seen from this point it is more massive and of less elegant shape than from most others. It looked like an enormous

On the lower part of the Mittèlegi ridge on the Eiger, high above the steep slopes of the northeast side, on September 10, 1921 the Japanese climber Yuko Maki, together with mountain guides Fritz Amatter, Fritz Steuri, and Samuel Brawand, was the first person to succeed in climbing this beautiful ridge. Climbing the steepest part is easier today because stationary ropes have been installed.

bastion, with an angle turned towards us. Whether I was absorbed in the worship of this noblest of alpine peaks, or whether the clouds had concealed much of the rest of the panorama, or whether we were thinking too much of the ascent that was to come, or whether, as I rather believe, the view is really an inferior one, certain it is that I thought very little of it. 'And what philosophical observations did you make?' will be the enquiry of one of those fanatics who, by a reasoning process to me utterly inscrutable, have somehow irrevocably associated alpine travelling with science. To them I answer, that the temperature was approximately (I had no thermometer) 212° (Fahrenheit) below freezing point. As for ozone, if any existed in the atmosphere, it was a greater fool than I take it for. As we had, unluckily, no barometer, I am unable to give the usual information as to the extent of our deviation from the correct altitude; but the Federal map fixes the height at 13,855 feet. Twenty minutes of freezing satisfied me with the prospect, and I willingly turned to the descent. I will not trouble my readers with a repetition in inverse order of the description of our previous adventures. I will not tell at length how I was sometimes half-suspended like a bundle of goods by the rope; how I was sometimes curled up into a ball, and sometimes stretched over eight or nine feet of rock; how the rope got twisted round my legs and arms and body, into knots which would have puzzled the Davenport Brothers; how, at one point, I conceived myself to be resting entirely on the point of one toe upon a stone coated with ice, and fixed very loosely in the face of a tremendous cliff, whilst Melchior absurdly told me I was 'ganz sicher,' and encouraged me to jump; how Jacob seemed perfectly at his ease; how Grove managed to lend a hand whenever I wanted one; and how Melchior, rising into absurdly high spirits, pirouetted and capered and struck attitudes on the worst places, and, in short, indulged himself in a display of fancy mountaineering as a partial relief to his spirits. We reached the snow safely at 1.15 P.M., and looked back triumphantly at the nastiest piece of climbing I had ever accomplished. The next traveller who makes the ascent will probably charge me with exaggeration. It is, I know, very difficult to avoid giving just cause for that charge. I must therefore apologise beforehand, and only beg my anticipated critic to remember two things: one, that on the first ascent a mountain, in obedience to some mysterious law, always is more difficult than at any succeeding ascent; secondly, that nothing can be less like a mountain at one time than the same mountain at another. The fresh snow and the bitter gale told heavily in the scale against us. Some of the hardest ascents I remember have been up places easy in fine weather, but rendered difficult by accidental circumstances. Making allowance, however, for this, I still believe that the last rocks of the Rothhorn will always count among the decidedly *mauvais pas* of the Alps.

We ran rapidly down the snow without much adventure, except that I selected the steepest part of the snow arête to execute what, but for the rope, would have been a complete somersault—an involuntary but appropriate per-

92

formance. Leaving the stony base of the Besso well to our right, we struck the route from the Trift-Joch at the point where a little patch of verdure behind a moraine generally serves for a halting and feeding-place. Here we stretched ourselves luxuriantly on the soft green moss in the afternoon sun. We emptied the last drops of the wine bag, lighted the pipe of peace—the first that day—and enjoyed the well-earned climbers' reward. Some mountaineers do not smoke—such is the awful darkness which lurks amidst our boasted civilisation. To them the words I have just read convey no sympathetic thrill. With the ignorance of those who have never shared a blessing, they probably affect even to despise the pleasure it confers. I can, at any rate, say that I have seldom known a happier half-hour than that in which I basked on the mossy turf in the shadow of the conquered Rothhorn—all my internal sensation of present comfort, of hard-won victory, and of lovely scenery, delicately harmonised by the hallowing influence of tobacco. We enjoyed what the lotos-eaters would have enjoyed, had they been making an ascent of one of the 'silent pinnacles of aged snow,' instead of suffering from sea-sickness, and partaking of a less injurious stimulant than lotos. Melchior pointed out during our stay eleven different ways of ascending the hitherto unconquered Grand Cornier. Grove and Jacob speculated on adding its summit also to our trophies, whilst I observed, not without secret satisfaction, that the gathering clouds would enforce at least a day's rest. We started homewards with a reluctant effort. I diversified the descent by an act of gallantry on my own account. Melchior had just skipped over a crevasse and turned to hold out a hand. With a contemptuous wave of my own I put his offer aside, remarking something about people who had done the Rothhorn. Next moment I was, it was true, on the other side of the crevasse, but, I regret to say, flat on my back, and gliding rapidly downwards into its depths. Melchior ignominiously hooked me under the arm with his axe and jerked me back, with a suitable warning for the future. We soon left the glacier, and on descending the path towards Zinal

It is 3:00 at night. Mountaineers leave the Rottal shelter (2,755 meters) to climb the Jungfrau. In the southwest the moon slowly sinks behind the Tschingelhorn (3,577 meters). On the watershed between the white Lütschine, Kander, and Lonza, the Tshingelhorn rises like a steep rocky cone which is covered with ice on its north and east sides. It was climbed for the first time on September 4, 1865 by the Rev. W. H. Hawker with mountain guides Ulrich and Christian Lauener and Heinrich Feuz.

93

were exposed to the last danger of the day. Certain natives had sprung apparently from the bowels of the earth, and hailed us with a strange dialect, composed in equal proportions of French, German, and Italian patois. Not understanding their remarks, I ran onwards, when a big stone whizzed close past my head. My first impression was that I was about to be converted into the victim of another Zinal murder, the gentleman by whom the last was committed being, as it was reported, still wandering amongst the mountains. I looked up, and saw that the offender was one of a large herd of cows, which were browsing in the charge of the natives, and managed, by kicking down loose stones, to keep up a lively fire along some distance of our path. We ran on all the faster, reached the meadows, and ascended the path to the village. Just as we reached the first houses, a melancholy figure advanced to meet us. Friendly greetings, however, proceeded from its lips, and we were soon shaking hands with poor Macdonald. We reached M. Epinay's inn at 6:45 P.M., the whole expedition occupying 16 h. 50 m. including about two hours' halts. A pleasant dinner succeeded, notwithstanding the clatter of sundry German tourists, who had flooded the little coffee-room and occupied my beloved sofa, and who kept up a ceaseless conversation. Soon afterwards, Macdonald having generously abandoned to me the cupboard in which he slept, I was trying to solve the problem of placing a length of six feet on a bed measuring about 3 ft. 6 in. by 2 ft. As its solution appeared to me to be inextricably mixed up with some question about the highest rocks of the Rothhorn, and as I heard no symptoms of my neighbour's slumbers in the next cupboard, which was divided from mine by a sort of paper partition, I incline to think that I was not long awake.

Alphonse Daudet (1840–1897) The French author Daudet created one of literature's classic comic characters in Tartarin de Tarascon, *the story of a lovable braggart and bonviveur from the south of France.* Tartarin sur les Alpes, *written in 1886, follows Tartarin and his friends on their hilarious journey through the Alps, including this climb of the Jungfrau.*

7 ALPHONSE DAUDET
The Ascent of the Jungfrau

There was a tremendous crowd that morning at the Belle Vue Hotel on the Little Scheideck. Notwithstanding the rain and the squalls, the tables had been laid out of doors, under the shelter of the veranda, amongst an assemblage of alpenstocks, fiasks, telescopes, cuckoo-clocks, etc.; and the tourists could, while breakfasting, gaze to the left upon the valley of Grindelwald, some 6000 feet below; on the right the Lauterbrunnen valley, and in front of them, at what seemed within gun-shot distance, the pure and stupendous slopes of the Jungfrau, with its *nevé,* its glaciers, the whiteness of it all illuminating the air around, making the glasses still more transparent and the table-linen still more snowy.

But for the moment the attention of the company was directed to a noisy bearded party of tourists, who were coming up on mule-back, on donkey-back, one man even in a *chaise à porteurs,* who prepared themselves for the ascent, by a copious breakfast; they were in high spirits, and the noise they made contrasted greatly with the worn-out and solemn airs of the Rice and Prune factions, some illustrious members of which had assembled at the Scheideck: Lord Chippendale, the Belgian Senator and his family, the Austro-Hungarian diplomatist and his family. It seemed as if all these bearded people were about to attempt the ascent, for they occupied themselves in turn with the preparations for departure, rose, hurried off to give instructions to the guides; to inspect the provisions, and from one end of the terrace to the other they shouted to each other in discordant accents,—

"*Hé!* Placide, see if the frying-pan is in the bag, and don't forget the spirit-lamp, mind!"

When the starting time arrived, however, it was perceived that all this was on account of one, and that of all the party one individual alone was going to undertake the ascent! But what an individual!

"Children, are we ready?" said the good Tartarin, in a triumphant and

95

joyful tone, which did not tremble with the shadow of a fear for the possible perils of the journey, his last doubt concerning the "machinery" of the Swiss having been dissipated that morning before the two Grindelwald glaciers, each provided with a turn-stile and a *guichet* with an inscription, "Entrance to the glacier, one franc and a half."

He could then enjoy this departure without regret: the delight of feeling himself the observed of all observers; envied, admired, by those cheeky little girls with the close-cropped hair, who had laughed at him so quietly on the Rigi-Kulm; and who were at that very moment in raptures, comparing that little man with that enormous mountain which he was going to ascend. One was sketching him in her album, another was requesting the honour of holding his alpenstock. "Tchimppegne—Tchimppegne," suddenly cried a lanky, melancholy Englishman, of brick-tint who was approaching with a bottle and a glass in his hands. Then, after having compelled the hero to drink, he said,—

"Lord Chippendale, sir; *et vô?*"

"Tartarin de Tarascon."

"Oh, yes,—Tarterine. It's a capital name for a horse," said his lordship, who must have been a great sportsman on the other side of the Channel!

The Austro-Hungarian diplomatist also came forward to shake the mountaineer by the hand between his mittens—having a vague recollection of having met him somewhere. "Delighted, delighted," he repeated many times, and, not knowing how to get out of it, he added: "My compliments to Madame,"—his society formula, by which he concluded all introductions.

But the guides were becoming impatient. The cabin of the Alpine Club must be reached before dark; there they would sleep, and there was not a moment to lose. Tartarin quite understood this, and saluted the company with a wave of his hand, smiled paternally at the malicious "misses," and then, in a voice of thunder, cried,—

"Pascalon, the banner!"

It was displayed, the Southerners had unfolded it, for they like theatrical display; and at the thirtieth repetition of *"Vive le Président!" "Vive Tartarin!"*

The Alp shepherd family Kühne sits at the lunch table on the Alp Tersol in the Calfeisen valley of St. Gallen. The tatsch *steams from a pan, which has been attached to a plank. The* tatsch, *made out of flour, water, salt, and butter is a popular dish among the residents of the Alps and is served with hot milk-coffee.*

"Ha! ha! *fen dé brut,*" the party started—the two guides in front carrying the *sac,* the provisions, and some wood; then Pascalon, holding the "oriflamme;" and the P.C.A. with the delegates, who were to escort him to the Guggi glacier, brought up the rear. So the procession deployed, the folds of the flag flapping upon the swampy ground, or on the naked or snowy crests, the *cortège* in a vague way recalling *le jour des morts* in country places.

Suddenly, the Commandant cried out in great alarm,—

"*Ve!* oxen!

They perceived some cattle grazing amid the undulations of the ground. The old warrior had a nervous terror of cows—an insurmountable fear; and as

Snow melting near the huts of Säss on the Brandlis mountain, with the Zinerspitz in the background. The huts are stacked over one another and protected at the rear against avalanches by a wall of stones.

97

his friends could not leave him alone, the delegation was obliged to halt. Pascalon handed the banner to one of the guides; then a last embrace, a few hurried words of warning, with their eyes on the cows,—

"Adieu, qué!"

"No imprudence, mind!"

And they parted.

As for any one proposing to ascend with the President, it was not to be thought of. The ascent was too high, *boufre!* As one got nearer to it, it seemed more difficult, the ravines increased, the peaks bristled up in a white chaos which seemed impossible to traverse. It was much better worth while to watch the ascent from the Scheideck.

Naturally, Tartarin in all his life had never set foot on a glacier. There were no such things upon the hillocks of Tarascon, which were as perfumed and dry as a bundle of bent-grass. Yet the surroundings of the Guggi gave him a sensation of familiarity, as if he had seen them before—arousing the memory of the chase in Provence, all around the Camargue, towards the sea. It was the same grass, but shorter and burnt up as if scorched by fire. Here and there were pools of water, infiltrations, indicated by slim reeds; then the moraine, like a mobile hill of sand, broken shells, and cinders; then the glacier, with its blue-green waves, tipped with white, undulating as a silent and frozen sea. The wind also had all the coolness and freshness of the seabreeze.

"No thanks; I have my *crampons*," said Tartarin, as the guide offered him woolen foot-protectors to wear over his boots: "Kennedy's pattern *crampons*— first-rate—very convenient." He shouted all this at the top of his voice as if the guide were deaf, so as to make him understand better, for Christian Inebnit knew no more French than his comrade Kaufmann. Then Tartarin seated himself upon the moraine and fixed upon his boots with irons the species of large pointed socks called *crampons.*

He had experimented a hundred times with these "Kennedy *crampons,*" and had tried them in the garden where the baobab grew; nevertheless the result was unexpected. Beneath the hero's weight the spikes buried themselves in the ice to

The marmot is one of our most lovable inhabitants of the Alps. Deep under the earth and cushioned in its cave with hay, it spends the six winter months in to protect itself from the inclemency and harshness of the mountain winter. Its natural enemy is man, who has exterminated the marmot in many regions of the Alps. Fortunately for the pleasure of mountain hikers, there are today imposing Munggen colonies in areas in the Säntis region, where a hundred years ago no animals were to be seen.

such a depth that all attempts to extricate them were vain! Behold Tartarin nailed to the ice, springing, swearing, making semaphores of his arms and alpenstock; and finally reduced to recall his guides, who had gone on ahead in the full belief that they had to do with an experienced climber!

Finding it impossible to pull him up, they unfastened the *crampons* from him, and left them in the ice, replacing them by a pair of worsted boot-coverings. The President then continued his way, not without toil and fatigue. Unaccustomed to use his *bâton,* he knocked it against his legs; the iron slid away from him, dragging him with it, when he leaned on it too heavily; then he tried the ice-axe, which proved even more difficult to manage; the swellings of the glacier increased, casting up its motionless waves into the appearance of a furious ocean suddenly petrified.

Apparently motionless only—for the loud crackings, the interior rumblings, the enormous blocks of ice slowly displaced like the revolving scenes at a theatre, displayed the action, the treacherousness, of this immense glacial mass; and before the climber's eyes, within reach of his axe, crevasses opened—bottomless pits into which the pieces of ice rolled to infinity. The hero fell into many of these traps—once up to his waist into one of the green gulfs, wherein his broad shoulders alone prevented him from being buried.

Seeing him so unskilful, and at the same time so calm and collected—laughing, singing, gesticulating, just as he had been doing at breakfast—the guides began to think that the Swiss champagne had got into his head. Could they think anything else of a President of an Alpine Club, of a mountaineer so renowned, of whom his companions never spoke without "Ah!" and expressive gestures? Having, therefore, seized him under his arms after the respectful fashion of policemen putting a well-born but elevated young gentleman into a cab, the guides, by the aid of monosyllables and gestures, endeavoured to arouse

Mountain goats with their young in the Alps near Jöchliturm. The ibex begin to separate from the herds in spring. The ibex herd wanders alone throughout summer. End of May and beginning of June is breeding time. The babies follow their mothers very easily even on the rocky slopes.

his reason to the dangers of the route; the threatening appearance of the crevasses, the cold, and the avalanches. With the points of their ice-axes they indicated the enormous accumulations of ice, the sloping wall of *névé* in front, rising to the zenith in a blinding glare.

But the worthy Tartarin laughed at all this. "*Ah! vaï, les crevasses!* Ah! get out with your avalanches!" and he choked with laughter, winked at the guides, and nudged them playfully in the ribs, to make them understand that he was in the secret as well as they!

The men ended by joining in the fun, carried away by Tarascon melody; and when they rested a moment upon a block of ice to permit "*monsieur*" to take breath, they "jodelled" in Swiss fashion, but not loudly, for fear of avalanches, nor for long, because time was passing apace. Evening was evidently coming on, the cold was becoming more intense, and the singular discoloration of the snows and the ice, heaped up and overhanging in masses, which, even under a cloudy sky, glitter and sparkle, but when daylight is dying out, gone up towards the tapering peaks, take the livid, spectral tints of the lunar world. Pallor, congelation, silence—all is dead. And the good Tartarin, so warm, so lively, began at length to lose his *verve,* when at the distant cry of a bird, the call of the "snow partridge" (ptarmigan) resounding amid the desolation, before his eyes there passed a vision of a burnt-up country, browned under a setting sun, sportsmen of Tarascon, wiping their foreheads, seated upon their empty game-bags, beneath the shade of an olive-tree! This reminiscence comforted him.

At the same time Kaufmann was pointing out to him something above them which looked like a faggot on the snow. This was the hut. It seemed as if a few paces would suffice to reach it, but it was a good half-hour ere they got there. One of the guides went on in front to light the fire. It was dark by this time; the east wind came piercingly off the death-like ground, and Tartarin, no longer troubling himself about anything, firmly sustained by the arm of the guide, jumped and bounded about until there was not a dry thread on him, notwithstanding the lowness of the temperature. Suddenly, a savoury odour of onion-soup assailed their nostrils.

They had reached the hut.

Nothing can be more simple than these stopping-places established on the mountains by the forethought of the Swiss Alpine Club; a single room, in which a sloping plank, serving as bed-place, occupies nearly all the space, leaving very little for the stove and the long table, which is nailed to the floor, as well as the benches which surround it. The supper was already laid when the men arrived; three bowls, tin spoons, the "Etna" for the coffee, two tins of Chicago preserved meats opened. Tartarin found the dinner excellent, although the onion-soup was rather smoked, and the famous patent lamp, which ought to have produced a quart of coffee in three minutes, failed to work.

For dessert they sang: it was the only way to converse with the guides. He

100

sang his country's songs: *la Tarasque, les Filles d'Avignon*. The guides responded with local songs in their German *patois*: "*Mi Vater isch en Appenzeller; aou, aou!*" Fine fellows these—hard as rock, with soft flowing beards like moss, clear eyes, accustomed to move in space, as sailors' are; and this sensation of the sea and space, which he had lately experienced while ascending the Guggi, Tartarin again experienced here in the company of these glacier-pilots in that narrow cabin, low and smoky, a veritable " 'tween-decks," in the dripping of the snow which the heat had melted on the roof, and the wild gusts of wind, like masses of falling water, shaking everything, making the planks creak and the lamp flicker: then suddenly stopping in a silence as if all the world were dead.

Mt. Jungfrau is illuminated by the evening sun above the veil of fog. The Rotbrett ridge (right) on the left border of this wall leads to Silverhorn (3,695 meters). The mountain climber reaches the Jungfrau peak (4,158 meters) by crossing Hochfirn. Gletscherhorn (3,983 meters) and Aletschhorn (4,195 meters) rise above Silverhorn, to the right of Ebnefluh (3,960 meters).

101

On the Alp Hohsass, on the way from the village of Simplon to Lagginbiwak of the Swiss women's alpine club, the mountain hiker views a special building. It consists of several sheep pens made from granite rocks. Here, on the Bartholomäus Day, the farmers of Simplon gather all their "muttini" to count them and mark their young.

Dinner was finished, when heavy steps were heard approaching, and voices were distinguished. A violent knocking at the door! Tartarin, somewhat alarmed, gazed at the guides. A nocturnal attack at such an elevation as this? The blows redoubled in intensity. "Who is there?" cried the hero, seizing his ice-axe: but the cabin was already invaded by two tall Americans masked in white linen, their clothing saturated with perspiration and snow-water, and behind them guides and porters—quite a caravan coming down from the summit of the Jungfrau.

"Welcome, my lords," cried Tartarin, with a hospitable and patronising wave of his hand, but "milords" had no compunction as to making themselves quite at home. In a few seconds the table was relaid, the bowls and spoons passed through some hot water to serve for the new-comers, according to the rules existing in all Alpine huts, the boots of "milords" were drying at the stove, while they, with their feet wrapped in straw, were disposing of a new supply of onion-soup.

These Americans were father and son—two ruddy giants, with the heads of pioneers, hard and practical. The older of the two seemed to have white eyes; and after a while the manner in which he tapped and felt around him, and the care which his son took of him, assured Tartarin that he was the famous blind mountaineer of whom he had heard at the Belle Vue Hotel, a fact he could scarcely credit, a famous climber in his youth, and who, notwithstanding his sixty years, had recommenced his ascents again with his son. He had in this manner already made the ascent of the Wetterhorn and the Jungfrau, and reckoned upon attacking the Cervin and Mont Blanc, declaring that the mountain air gave him intense enjoyment, and recalled all his former vigour.

"But," said Tartarin to one of the porters—for the Yankees were not communicative, and only replied "Yes" or "No" to all advances— "but, if he cannot see, how can he manage to cross dangerous places?"

102

"Oh, he has the foot of a true mountaineer, and his son looks after him, places his feet in the proper positions, etc. The fact is, he never has an accident."

"More especially as accidents are never very deplorable, *que?*" After a knowing smile to the astonished porter, the Tarasconnais, more and more persuaded that all this was *blague,* stretched himself on the plank, rolled himself in his rug, his comforter up to his eyes, and fell asleep, notwithstanding the light, the chatter, the smoke of pipes, and the smell of the onion-soup.

"*Mossié! Mossié!*" (Monsieur).

One of the guides was shaking him by the shoulder, while the other was pouring out some boiling coffee into the bowls.

There were a few oaths and some grumbling from the sleepers, as Tartarin pushed past them in his way to the table and to the door. All of a sudden, he found himself in the open air, shivering with cold, and puzzled by the moonlight upon the white plains, the frozen cascades, which the shadows of the peaks,

Behind the sheep folds of Hohsass, the majestic mountains of Fletschhorn-Lagginhorn Weissmies project into the sky. Below the 4,023-meter-high Weissmies one recognizes the beautifully formed side moraines of the Weissmies glacier.

aiguilles, and *seracs*, cut with intense blackness. There was not the bewildering scintillation of the afternoon, nor the livid grey tinge of the evening, but a town cut by dark alleys, mysterious passages, dubious angles between the marble monuments and crumbled ruins—a dead town with its wide deserted squares.

Two o'clock! With good walking they ought to reach the summit by mid-day. "*Zou*," said the P. C. A. quite gaily, and pressed forward to the assault. But the guides stopped him: it was necessary to rope themselves.

"Ah! go along with your tying up! Very well, then; if it amuses you, be it so!"

Christian Inebnit took the lead, leaving six feet of rope between him and Tartarin, and the same length between Tartarin and the other guide, who was carrying the provisions and the banner. The Tarasconnais got on better than the day before, and really he did not seem to appreciate the difficulties of the path— if the way along that terrible *arête* of ice can be called a path—over which they were advancing with the greatest caution. It was a few inches wide, and so slippery that Christian had to cut steps in it.

The *arête* glittered between profound abysses. But do you think Tartarin was afraid? Not a bit of it! Scarcely did he experience the little tremor of the newly-made Freemason who has to submit to the ordeal! He placed his feet exactly in the holes cut by the guide, doing everything as he saw him do it, as coolly as if he were in the baobab garden, walking on the edge of the fountain, to the great terror of the gold-fish. At one time, the crest became so narrow that they were compelled to proceed on all-fours, and while they were advancing slowly a tremendous detonation was heard on the right beneath them. "An avalanche!" said Inebnit, stopping quite still so long as the uproar lasted, while the reverberations, grandly repeated, terminated by a lengthened thunder-roll, which slowly died away in echoes. After that the former terrible silence succeeded, covering all things like a winding-sheet.

The *arête* passed, they reached the *névé*, which sloped easily, but was terribly long. They had climbed for more than an hour, when a thin streak of rosy hue began to touch the peaks high—very high—over their heads. Day was announcing its arrival. As a good Southerner, cherishing an enmity to darkness, Tartarin trolled out his cheerful song,—

Grand souleù de la Provenço
Gai compaire dou mistrau.

A tug at the cord both before and behind stopped him short in the middle of his verse: "Hush! hush!" cried Inebnit, indicating with the handle of his ice-axe the menacing line of immense and clustered *séracs* which the least shock would send down upon the travellers. But the Tarasconnais knew what he was about— they were not going to humbug him; so he recommenced in a resonant voice,—

The Gatterifirst (2,099 meters), a mountain ridge which connects the Kreuzberge in the west, offers a few superior climbing paths. The Rosakante has been chosen frequently in the last years. The mountain climber can observe the spectacle of a sunset in autumn from the highest point of the ridge.

From the Garschinafurgga, mountains above the Antön- ien Valley appear perfectly clear on a sultry autumn evening.

The guides, perceiving that they could not keep the headstrong singer within due bounds, made a wide *détour* to avoid the *séracs,* and soon were brought to a standstill by an enormous *crevasse,* which was lighted in its green depths by the first rays of daylight. A snow bridge crossed it, but so thin and fragile, that at the very first step it disappeared in a whirlwind of fine snow, dragging with it the head guide and Tartarin, who hung by the cord, which Rudolf Kaufmann, the rear guide, gripped with all his force, his axe firmly fixed in the snow to sustain the tension. But though he could hold up the men, he could not haul them out, and he stood crouching down, with clenched teeth and straining muscles, too far from the *crevasse* to perceive what was passing within it.

Astounded by the fall, and half blinded by the snow, Tartarin for a minute threw his legs and arms about like a puppet: but then, righting himself by means of the rope, he hung over the chasm, his nose touching the icy wall, which thawed beneath his breathing, in the posture of a plumber mending a water-pipe. He saw the sky paling above him, the last stars were disappearing; beneath him a chasm of intense darkness, whence ascended a cold air.

Nevertheless, his first astonishment over, he regained his coolness and good humour,—

"Eh! up there! Father Kaufmann, don't let us get mouldy here, *qué!* There is a draught, and this cursed cord is bruising our ribs."

Kaufmann was not able to reply. If he unlocked his teeth he would lose some of his strength. But Inebnit hailed from below,—

"*Mossié! Mossié!* ice-axe!"—for he had lost his own in the *crevasse;* and the heavy instrument passed from Tartarin's hands into those of the guide—a diffi-

107

cult operation because of the length of cord which separated them. The guide wanted it to cut steps in the ice in front of him, or to cling by it foot and hand.

The strain upon the rope being thus lessened by one half Rudolf Kaufmann, with carefully calculated force and infinite precautions, commenced to drag up the President, whose cap at length appeared over the edge of the *crevasse*. Inebnit came up in his turn, and the two mountaineers met with effusion, but with the few words which are exchanged after great dangers by people of a slow habit of speaking. They were much moved, and trembling with their exertions. Tartarin passed them his flask to restore them. He seemed quite composed and calm, and while he was beating the snow from his dress rhythmically, he kept humming a tune, under the very noses of the astonished guides.

"*Brav! brav! Franzose*," said Kaufmann, patting him on the shoulder, and Tartarin, with his jolly laugh, replied,—

"*Farceur*, I knew quite well there was no danger!"

Within the memory of the guide, never had there been such an Alpinist as this!

They continued their way, climbing a gigantic wall of ice eighteen hundred or two thousand feet high, in which they cut steps, which occupied much time.

The man of Tarascon began to feel his strength failing him under the blazing sun, which reflected all the whiteness of the landscape, all the more trying for his eyes as he had dropped his spectacles into the *crevasse*. Soon afterwards a terrible faintness seized upon him, that *"mal de montagnes"* which has the same effect as sea-sickness. Utterly done up, and light-headed, with dragging limbs, he stumbled about, so that the guides had to haul him along, one on each side, as they had done the day before, sustaining him, even drawing him up the ice-wall. Scarcely three hundred feet intervened between them and the top of the Jungfrau; but although the snow was firm and the way easy, this last stage occupied an "interminable" time, while the fatigue and the sensation of suffocation increased with Tartarin continually.

Suddenly, the guides let him go, and waving their hats began to "jodel" with delight. They had reached the summit. This point in immaculate space, this

The new Garschina-hut of the Rätia section of the SAC is built on Garschinafurgga on the foot of the rugged wall of rocks on Sulzfluh. It is a comfortable base not only for the mountain climber who looks for adventures in the mountain notches, but also for the mountain hiker, who can reach the peak of Sulzfluh easily without great risk. There is no service in Garschina-hut. It is not open all the time, as are most of the SAC huts, because of its proximity to the border. The key can be obtained from the border guard at St. Antönien or from the boarding house "Sulzfluh" on Partnum.

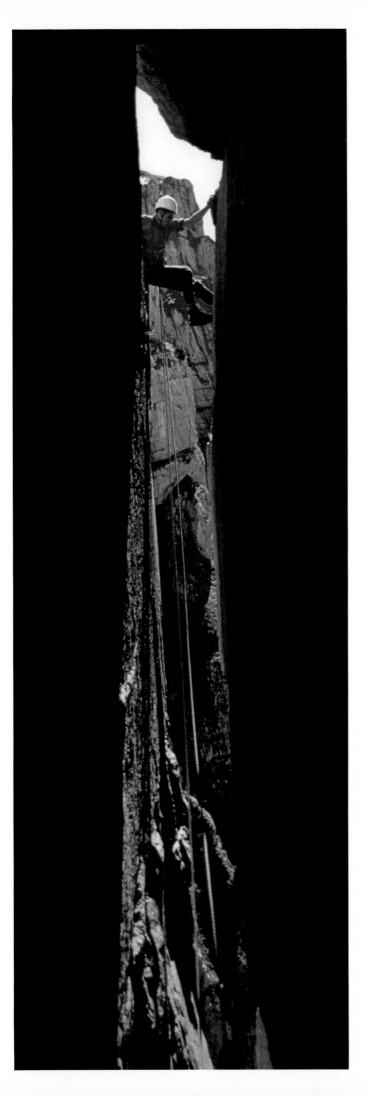

A very smooth stem-chimney divides the Ros-Church, an over eighty-meter-high detached tower on the foot of Chäserugg. The climb to the tower is very difficult on all routes.

A deep crack yawns in the thin ridge-wall, which connects the first and second Kreuzberg. The first climber of the roped party climbs deeper into the notch till he can reach the opposite side with a wide step. Climbing up is more difficult. Further members of the roped party often master the notch on the stretched and well-hooked double rope. This "small rope-way" on the "Ersten" is a classic climbing spot in the Kreuzberge.

white crest somewhat rounded, was the end, and for poor Tartarin the end of the torpor in which he had been walking, as in his sleep, for the last hour.

"Scheideck! Scheideck!" exclaimed the guides, pointing out to him far below on a verdant plateau, standing out from the mists of the valley, the Hotel Belle Vue, looking a very toy-house.

From there they had a magnificent panorama spread before them, a snow slope tinged with an orange glow by the sun, or a cold deep blue; a mass of ice fantastically sculptured into towers, steeples, needles, *arêtes;* gigantic mounds, like graves of the mastodon and the megatherium. All the colours of the rainbow played upon them, uniting again in the beds of the great glaciers, with their motionless ice-falls, crossed by tiny streams which the sun was warming into life again. But at the great elevation the reflections were toned down, a light was floating in the air, a cold ecliptic light, which made Tartarin shiver as much as the sensation of the silence and solitude of the white desert and its mysterious recesses.

A little smoke was perceived, and some detonations were heard from the hotel. They had seen the tourists, and were firing cannon in their honour, and the conviction that they saw him, that his Alpinists were there, the young ladies, the illustrious Rices and Prunes, with their opera-glasses, recalled Tartarin to the importance of his mission. He snatched the Tarascon banner from the hands of the guide, and waved it two or three times; then, fixing his ice-axe in the snow, he seated himself, upon the iron of the pick, flag in hand, superb, facing the public. And without his perceiving it—by one of those spectral images frequent at the tops of mountains, the result of sun, and of mist which was rising behind him—a gigantic Tartarin was outlined on the sky, enlarged and shortened, the beard bristling out of the comforter, like one of the Scandinavian deities, which tradition presents to us as enthroned in the midst of the clouds.

110

*Extreme climbing conditions
exist at big Hundsteinbauch
on the south wall of the
Hundstein in the Säntisre-
gion. The Furgglenfirst with
the tower-house in the background, behind it the peaks of
the Vorarlberg mountains,
and in the far distance the
Fählenlake. In the fall of
1965 mountain climbers
Max Kaufman, Heiner Kei-
mer, Sepp Henkel, Horst
Wenin, and Paul Wuest mastered the direct overhang-
route in several weeks of hard
struggle. In the Alps, this is
the most adventurous and
most daring climbing route.*

Edmund von Fellenberg (1838–1902) Bernese mountain engineer and naturalist Edmund von Fellenberg was the most successful pioneer in the Bernese Alps. He climbed all the important peaks between the Wild-strubel and the Wellhorn. He conquered many as the first climber and others by new and more difficult paths. One of the these was the Mönch, which he climbed over the steep Northwest-Bollwerk. Von Fellenberg was among the founders of the Swiss Alpen-club and was its first secretary.

8 EDMUND VON FELLENBERG

Mönch

Among mountain-climbing challenges of the inner Bernese Alps, none had greater attraction than trying to climb the Mönch. I had conquered the Jungfrau from the north side, so it was no longer either of great worth or pleasing to me. I had long held the anticipation that the old, jealous hermit would accept me hospitably—yes, that he would even be satisfied if I tugged at his grey beard and emptied a goblet on his cap in his honor.

The plans for the new climbing were laid by my worthy friend, H. B. George, from the Alpine Club, to whom is due the honor of having climbed the Jungfrau from the north side. He approached the Mönch first but was ungraciously rejected by the mountain. The attack failed for lack of time, insufficient preparation and auxiliary means, since George wanted to make the climb in one day. This is a pure impossibility, in that endless steps must be chopped time and time again in attempting the climb.

The attempt in the year 1862 showed, in spite of everything, that the climb would be possible if the bottom ledge of a steep, hanging glacier, which broke away from a rather high ice wall, was mounted by means of a long guide rope. The Englishman didn't come over this break in the ice and presumed correctly

The Tschierva hut (2,573 meters). The Bernina section of the SAC is the exit point for one of the most famous and beloved ridge tours in the Alps: the Crast'Alva or Bianco Ridge on Piz Bernina. Other well-loved tour destinations in the hut district are the Piz Roseg, Piz Scerscen, and Piz Morteratsch. Over the Tschierva Glacier, the Porta de Roseg is visible. It's a saddle between the Piz Roseg and Piz Scerscen.

A rescue mission in difficult terrain. Two climbers are being saved by a rescue column with help from steel-wire ropes, at the large overhang of the south wall of Hundstein. The steel-wire rope and rope winches were carried to the pinnacle by the rescue team. Two rescuers can be lowered to the spot of the accident on the five millimeter thick steel-wire rope. There they strap the unfortunate climbers into sling-type chairs and raise them to the peak. The rescue team on the wall speaks with the climbers about the sparkling view, in order to ease tension.

The Piz Bernina (4,049 meters) as seen from the Diavolezza. It is the highest mountain in Grison and the last 4,000-meter mountain in the East. It was first climbed in 1850 by topographer Johann Wilhelm Fortunat Coaz in connection with his surveys. His guides were Jon and Lorenz Ragut. For their climbing route they chose the east ridge, which is seldom traveled today. The easiest way to the peak leads over the Spalla, or south ridge (left of the peak). The most beautiful route leads over the perennial snow of the north ridge, which is known as Bianco Ridge or Crast'Alva to mountain climbers (to the right of the peak). Berlin professor Paul Güssfeldt first climbed this ridge path on August 12, 1878 with the native guides Hans Grass and Johann Gross.

that, if he did, the difficulty wouldn't let up. There was also in my thoughts a bit of revenge which drove me to this promising climb, since climbing the Jungfrau from the north side was no longer a priority with me. All one's emulated rivals willingly circle in triumphant friendship, and all rivalries are of a noble nature. The main purpose is, and remains, the challenge: to raise spirits and bodies, to harden one's self, to refresh, and to investigate in new directions our wonderful glacier world in its most inaccessible hiding places.

A third, and indeed determining, factor for me was the immovable contact line. In earlier climbs this was precisely fastened to the north front of the Mönch between the lime formation and the primitive rocks. We kept our plan as secret as possible. The twenty-five-foot-long, brand-new ladder was carried to the Wengeralp at night in the mist in order not to attract attention and in order to deceive people about our plans. As the morning of July 11 finally arrived with a lovely northeast wind and cool, cloudless air, there was nothing more holding us in the valley. And at 10:30 A.M. we departed. Where? Nobody knew!

In great heat we climbed the Wengeralp to the flowery pastureland. Since Gertsch arrived the day before with the huge ladder, the townspeople naturally asked him where we were going. Gertsch pretended not to know and everyone assumed we had the Jungfrau in mind again. We also left the good people in doubt over our destination. We ate quickly, loaded two days provisions, and departed at 4:30 P.M. Gertsch carried the ladder, and Peter Egger and Christian Michel divided the rest of the load. My tent and a large travel rug formed the main equipment for the bivouac which we had decided to occupy. With quick steps we crossed the cow pastures and sheep meadows to the Eiger glacier. We traversed the bottommost ledge of it and climbed the endless spoil banks and rocky ledges which cover the floor of the Mönch above the Eiger glacier. As we climbed over the lowest pile of rocks, we bowed a bit to the left instead of going straight up to the Guggi glacier, which was the path to the Silberhorn.

We stopped partway up for a short pause on the steeply piled rocks. Scree with scanty *Ranunculus glacialis, Saxifraga oppositifolia,* and *Thalaspi rotundifolium* growing on it contrasted with rock benches and crumbling slate slopes. Snow flurries, a snow field, and then rock again quickly brought us to the heights. As it began to darken, we looked for a flat place at the foot of a belt of rocks. We were about 3,000 meters high, and flat rock lay all around us. A little cooking hearth was quickly built, the tent erected, and the large travel rug spread out. Until the chocolate was finished, we sat in front of the tent and enjoyed a pipe and conversation about the splendid summer evening. Soon the valleys lay in shadows, and a few blue streaks of haze lingered over the Thunersee and the flatlands. The orange-colored evening sky was lost at the zenith in the total spectrum of yellow, green, and blue. And in the dark grey-blue of the night sky, one star after another began to appear. At nine o'clock we lay down and immediately fell asleep.

116

At three o'clock on the morning of July 12, Gertsch crept out of the tent to prepare breakfast. Half an hour later we were wide awake. Gertsch took the coarse, heavy, long ladder, and at four o'clock we set out. The morning was above criticism; there wasn't a single cloud in the sky, and a sharp, cold breeze drove us on. The rocks over our sleeping area were steeper, and the gaps between them wider. We therefore turned left to the ridge of the cliff over the Eiger glacier. Here we could move more easily. We were still on the ridge that buckles out of the north side of the Mönch itself. This ridge turns to wide, level fields of lime as it nears the Eiger glacier. This outer portion of the powerful mountain encloses a desolate, wild caldron whose chaotic ice masses nearly cause numerous glacial faults and avalanches which could separate the glacier from the mountain. The glacial cauldron is near to the Eiger glacier, which begins at the Eiger pass. The rocks became steeper and steeper, and the smooth lime surfaces afforded little standing space, especially since they were covered in part with a transparent ice crust.

Poor Gertsch had trouble with his precious, colossal ladder. He climbed everywhere with it, and the ladder was so heavy that he often stumbled.

When he wasn't on the rope, he risked great danger to his life. Every few seconds we checked where the large monstrosity stood or lay, so that Gertsch wouldn't risk more than a few steps unobserved. Position-wise, the ladder had to be pulled after him. In short, it was a very tiring and time-consuming maneuver. Further up the rocks became lighter, and around seven o'clock we encountered the first snow from previous years. This snow covered the lime rock as a steep ridge and bound the outerworks with the Mönch itself. Soon afterwards the step-chopping began, and we had to work for a good half hour before we could stand on the snow ridge. From this place we got our first glance at the steepness of the perennial snow and the threatening, overhanging glacier which suddenly appeared and seemed to make further progress impossible.

From the Lischanna hut this is a view of the lower region on a late autumn evening. Down below, in the valley, is the tiny village of Ftan, which lies above the Inns ravine on a sunny terrace.

117

By climbing the Piz Bernina over the Bianco Ridge, the mountain climber enjoys the world from a birds-eye view. The Morterasch Glacier extends under him. At the foot of Bernina are the broken glacial chunks from Morterasch—the labyrinth. The Pers glacier flows toward the valley from Piz Palü and then flows into the lower part of Isla Persa in the Morterasch Glacier.

Above the right bank of the Pers Glacier is the Diavolezza, the end station of a rope lift and a world famous view.

For fifteen minutes we worked lustily on a nearly level ridge, but then it began to get steeper. The snow, however, remained so good that we could go approximately a hundred feet without having to hack a step. Then the shining ice appeared, glistening in the sun, and the endless chopping began. Step after step had to be chopped to sufficient width. Gertsch, with the long ladder, could hardly maintain his equilibrium.

After an hour we didn't see a single rock. As Gertsch laid the ladder down, the physical strain caught up with him, and he fell unconscious and chalk-white to the ground.

After the poor man vomitted vehemently and took a good dose of Hoffmann's Drops, he said he was prepared to risk going further. At first it went well, but then we went back to chopping, and the ice wall became still steeper. Gertsch had to practically be pulled step by step, although Egger had taken the ladder from him. We now strove to mount a gneiss rock somewhat to the right since directly ahead the ice slope was too steep. Under us, to the right, the glistening, smooth ice wall dropped off into the precipices of the Guggi. The gallant Christen again took the ice axe in his hand, and, under weighty blows, the splinters flew. Suddenly Michel turned around, and with a frightening scream of anger he guided poor Gertsch, who had fallen asleep in his steps, against a 45°-hanging chunk of ice. "If we should all fall together into eternity, it's your fault!" With effort and danger, in great trepidation for Gertsch's life and our own well-being, we spent a terrible half hour. During this time Gertsch drifted in and out of sleep while making dangerous vertical steps. We had hardly reached a safe area when Gertsch fell asleep as if unconscious. It had already been ten hours, and the deciding ice wall was still high over us!

Only at this point could we begin to see the impossibility of reaching the zenith that day. Gertsch was practically ineffective. To let him descend alone

118

would make me responsible for a human life, for, in his condition, he would never reach the bottom alive. Therefore, we had to be satisfied for this day with a reconnaissance mission. Gertsch was left in a safe place on sunny rocks, with a knapsack as a pillow and my travel rug as a blanket.

In addition, we left him some provisions and wine in case he recovered sufficiently to enjoy them. Recovery was also necessary for us, so we forced down some food before giving Gertsch the positive order not to move from the place until we returned.

First Egger took the ladder while the older Christian Michel chopped the steps with the strength of a young man. This was necessary since from the gneiss rock to the overhanging glacier there is an ice wall at a 45°-48° angle. George, who during his attempt at the Mönch took delight in counting the steps he chopped, had counted at least 500 by the time he reached the bottom of this ice wall. During the monotonous chopping Michel assured me he had done much in

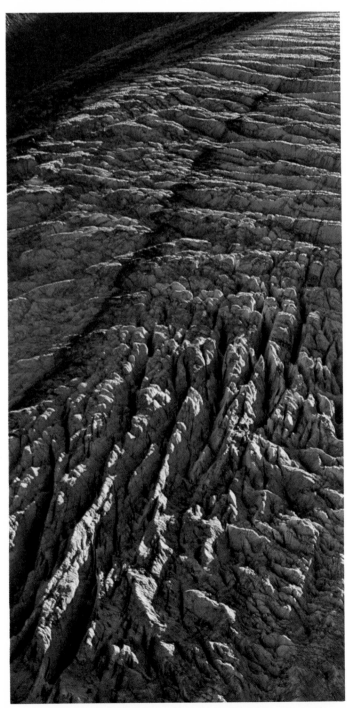

The rock bed of a glacier defines the speed of the flow and the form of the ice masses. Over a hump of rock, the more-or-less compact ice masses of the Pers Glacier break apart. Oblique, long edge splinters are formed. It is a chaos of clefts and towers.

119

his forty years of glacier experience, but that he had never been as terrified as when he saw Gertsch sleeping against the step. One tiny bump to the right, and all of us would have flown hopelessly into the depths. Halfway up the terrible overhang Egger took the lead and Michel took the monstrous ladder. It was 12:10 P.M., and we had climbed up the more than forty-foot-high ice wall with our noses extended into the blue heaven. There we were. Directly behind us was the ice ridge, the bottom of which Gertsch nearly fell from. To our right we could see steep ice walls extended by falling chunks of ice from the hanging Guggi glacier. To our left was a frightfully steep ice wall also extended from the blue walls of the hanging glacier. In front of us was vertical ice. With a jokingly spoken curse about the ladder, which we hadn't needed so far, Michel placed it deep under the ice wall so that we could make loops to keep from falling. "Now, Fellenberg, keep yourself still, and don't move from this place! Let the line out! I'll pay close attention to keeping us safe." And so Christian Michel led the best reconnaissance mission that ever a leader guided.

My English rope was thirty-five meters long. To this Egger's rope was knotted tightly at approximately eighteen meters. I took my place on the ladder under the ice wall, and Egger went quietly past me to the edge of a particularly steep piece of hanging ice which had fallen from the Eiger Glacier. Now Michel tied himself to the end of the powerful rope and began to notch out places for hands and feet from the frightfully steep slope of the glacier. From where I stood he looked like a fly clinging to the wall. The rope was slowly let out by his command, and it was held tightly by Egger and me. Soon Michel disappeared behind an ice projection. We sat there silently in anxious anticipation, inwardly terrified for the life of our guide. If Michel considered it necessary to scout the full length of the rope, he would certainly do it in the interest of success. Nearly half an hour passed before Michel was visible again, and soon afterwards we grasped each other's hands happily. The news was encouraging. There was still a wall to be climbed, and further up there was a "ÿschwändli" (omen), put there by "en Tüfels Hackery" ("the devil's chopping"). Nevertheless, he was in good spirits.

Now we enjoyed our noon meal in a quiet, serene frame of mind. The remaining rope was rolled up, and at one o'clock we started down the path back to Gertsch. We left our long yet too short, annoying, dangerous ladder behind at the ice wall. Naturally we were happy that we never needed it. By two o'clock we were back to Gertsch who was quite recovered. And since we didn't have the ladder to carry any longer, he could be watched closely in regard to falling asleep. With luck we came down quickly, so that by three o'clock, we had arrived at our sleeping place. Here we rested for the remainder of the afternoon, and all of us slept in the sun. Then we held a council and decided to take all the necessary provisions to the zenith the following day. Gertsch, on the other hand,

120

An Alpine mountain climber climbs on the perennial snow of Crast' Alva as if on a heavenly ladder leading to the peak. The perennial snow ridge ends on Piz Alva, the 3,995-meter-high front peak of Bernina. Often the most difficult part of the climb begins there. The descent from Bernina begins there, and the ascent to the peak from this point is dangerous in freezing weather and hard work in loose snow.

was to be sent home with the tent, blanket, and all superfluous provisions.

Since it was so early, Gertsch was sent to the Wengeralp to fetch the supplies. The thought of not having to join us the next morning gave him his full strength and health, and we saw him climbing down the rocks with remarkable ease. On the Wengeralp they thought we were dead until Gertsch arrived and brought the news of the continuing bivouac. At eight o'clock, with night upon us, Gertsch returned and said that many bets were made for and against the success of the mission. . . .

On Friday, July 13 the three of us were in good spirits. The next day promised to be splendid and cloudless, the night was just as mild and clear as the previous one, and our hope had turned to near certainty. Today is here and never again!

We set out at 3:30 A.M. We hoped today to descend possibly in the depths of the Eiger or to Faulberg. I'll tell nothing more of the ascent up the ice wall. Since

Gateway to the glacier at Turtmann; the beginning of the waterfall at Turtmann. In the summer and fall, parts of the glacier swallow up gravel and dirt and give the glacier a grey, dirty appearance.

122

all the steps had been previously chopped, we reached the top by 7:00. Michel went out again to the terrible place over the abyss and under the ice wall to improve the notches for our hands and feet. Then forward! I confess that I hung out over the abyss with great shuddering and clutched at the notches for hands and feet. Walking sideways, we had to feel for the steps, at the perpendicular ice wall for the finger holes, and at the 60°-inclined ice slope for the foot holes. Between our clutching limbs the view plunged without interruption 2000 feet deep into the wild Eiger caldron. Its yawning crevices seemed to invite us to tumble down. Under the eternally serene command of Christian at the beginning and then the end of the rope, I traversed the most terrible place that I ever encountered. It was a place in which one must have a quiet pulse and a cool head.

Now we stood in front of an indentation in the ice wall, the remnant of an old collapsed crevice. Without chopping one step we climbed fifteen minutes in the snow and reached the top of the wall whose power we had learned to respect....

High above us now stood a second ice wall, the lowest part of which must have been fifteen meters high. With luck it wouldn't be protruding, but it was nearly vertical. I dug a deep hole in the wall of piled-up powdery snow with my foot while Michel grasped the ice wall with the strength of a giant. Here large steps would have to be chopped out and hand holes cut as additional help. Egger always stood one step lower than Michel to help keep his balance with the ice axe. I scrambled up with my hands and feet in the irregular steps, held mightily from above. Then the provisions followed, and finally Egger.

It was 9:10 A.M. In front of us was a steep slope of perennial snow. There were many more steps to be chopped. Then we stood at the edge of a monstrous crevice which was totally snow-filled. Its upper wall promised to be quite tiring. While we were looking at the new difficulty, there was a sharp thunderclap followed by a long rolling.

While climbing the Piz Scerscen (3,971 meters) from the Tschierva hut, the alpine climber has to surmount a chunk of ice broken away from a glacier. This can be an extremely difficult task.

123

A large ice mass broke away from the fault at the left. It crackled, rumbled, and scattered powerfully into the dreadful depths of the glacier. We imagined arriving at the ridge and finally being at the plateau of the protruding glacier. But there was no way. Immediately afterwards we saw a long slope of perennial snow above us. Two hours of chopping steps would be spent before we could stand on a lovely snow floor again. We would then have topped a rather steep ice wall which extends from the western tip of the Mönch peak to the Jungfrau pass. We would have to head towards this for the nearest rocks were far away, and the ice wall inadvisable.

"Now we have won!" the leader rejoiced. We all rejoiced!...

After a fifteen-minute pause we started out again. It was 12:20. The crevice which separated the snow floor from the ice wall gave us much to do. After long chopping in the shining ice, we turned right towards the farthest rocks on the Mönch ridge. With a glance we looked out over the vassals of the Finsteraar and Aletschhorn, the great Aletsch, the Jungfrau, and all our old, beloved friends. And forward to our highest goal!

The rocks above were dangerous, rather narrow ridges. The good rock afforded safety to our climbing, and it was a welcome change after climbing in ice steps for so long. Naturally we stayed on the rock as much as possible, since the ice wall had no more snow and was much too steep. At 2:45 we reached a point at which the two forks of the west ridge joined. One was the fork we climbed up, the other plunged directly into the perennial snow on the Jungfrau. We left our packs here. There was still about fifteen minutes of rock ridge followed by some snow which ended in a monstrous point. We had to mount this point and now saw, for the first time, that the ridge reached its highest point a few hundred feet away. We hurried forward restlessly. The ridge broadened to a snow-filled platform whose three corners formed a raised bump. The highest was the northeast. Amidst cheers and jubilant oaths we planted the flag at this point. The Mönch was conquered at 3:30. We had used exactly twelve hours to go from the bivouac to the peak, despite chopping steps.

There was a moderate east wind. The temperature was 3° Centigrade in the sun and 2° in the shade. This was all very pleasant. Unfortunately, we had only a glance here and there through the billowing fog.

We left the peak at four o'clock, and by five o'clock we were back to our packs. From there we climbed to the ridge which led immediately to the Jungfrau pass. We climbed down through a protected gap in the rock where earlier Mönch climbers had spent the night. Without blankets or provisions and despite the wet and heat, we spent the long night on the rock. On July 14 we stumbled with stiff joints over the Mönch pass, the Fiescher wall, and the hospitable Bäregg. We carried triumph and joy in our hearts.

Mark Twain (1835–1910) The American Samuel Langhorne Cle-
mens, who wrote under the pseudonym Mark Twain, was one of the
great comic writers of world literature, famous for his sarcasm and
exaggerated humor. Readers especially enjoyed his stories of traveling
through Europe. This description of the Rigi is from A Tramp
Abroad, *published in 1880.*

9 MARK TWAIN

A Trip to the Rigi Mountains

The Rigi-Kulm is an imposing Alpine mass, 6,000 feet high, which stands by itself, and commands a mighty prospect of blue lakes, green valleys, and snowy mountains—a compact and magnificent picture three hundred miles in circumference. The ascent is made by rail, or horseback, or on foot, as one may prefer. I and my agent panoplied ourselves in walking costume, one bright morning, and started down the lake on the steamboat; we got ashore at the village of Wäggis, three quarters of an hour distant from Lucerne. This village is at the foot of the mountain.

We were soon tramping leisurely up the leafy mule-path, and then the talk began to flow, as usual. It was twelve o'clock noon, and a breezy, cloudless day; the ascent was gradual, and the glimpses, from under the curtaining boughs, of blue water, and tiny sail boats, and beetling cliffs, were as charming as glimpses of dreamland. All the circumstances were perfect—and the anticipations, too, for we should soon be enjoying, for the first time, that wonderful spectacle, an Alpine sunrise—the object of our journey. There was (apparently) no real need to hurry, for the guide-book made the walking distance from Wäggis to the summit only three hours and a quarter. I say "apparently," because the guide-book had already fooled us once,—about the distance from Allerheiligen to Oppenau,—and for aught I knew it might be getting ready to fool us again. We were only certain as to the altitudes,—we calculated to find out for ourselves how many hours it is from the bottom to the top. The summit is 6,000 feet above the sea, but only 4,500 feet above the lake. When we had walked half an hour, we were fairly into the swing and humor of the undertaking, so we cleared for action; that is to say, we got a boy whom we met to carry our alpenstocks and satchels and overcoats and things for us; that left us free for business.

I suppose we must have stopped oftener to stretch out on the grass in the shade and take a bit of a smoke than this boy was used to, for presently he asked

125

Crossing the Diablons (3,609 meters), the mountain massif between Tal and Zinal, with many glaciers on its north side, is a very rewarding tour. The view from the 4,000 -meter-high mountain is overwhelming. A view from the Tal hut to the Diablon.

if it had been our idea to hire him by the job, or by the year? We told him he could move along if he was in a hurry. He said he wasn't in such a very particular hurry, but he wanted to get to the top while he was young. We told him to clear out, then, and leave the things at the uppermost hotel and say we should be along presently. He said he would secure us a hotel if he could, but if they were all full he would ask them to build another one and hurry up and get the paint and plaster dry against we arrived. Still gently chaffing us he pushed ahead, up the trail, and soon disappeared. By six o'clock we were pretty high up in the air, and the view of lake and mountains had greatly grown in breadth and interest. We halted a while at a little public house, where we had bread and cheese and a quart or two of fresh milk, out on the porch, with the big panorama all before us, —and then moved on again.

Ten minutes afterward we met a hot, red-faced man plunging down the mountain, with mighty strides, swinging his alpenstock ahead of him and taking a grip on the ground with its iron point to support these big strides. He stopped, fanned himself with his hat, swabbed the perspiration from his face and neck with a red handkerchief, panted a moment or two, and asked how far it was to Wäggis. I said three hours. He looked surprised, and said,—

"Why, it seems as if I could toss a biscuit into the lake from here, it's so close by. Is that an inn, there?"

I said it was.

"Well," said he, "I can't stand another three hours, I've had enough for to-day; I'll take a bed there."

I asked,—

"Are we nearly to the top?"

"Nearly to the *top!* Why, bless your soul, you haven't really started, yet."

I said we would put up at the inn, too. So we turned back and ordered a hot supper, and had quite a jolly evening of it with this Englishman.

126

The German landlady gave us neat rooms and nice beds, and when I and my agent turned in, it was with the resolution to be up early and make the utmost of our first Alpine sunrise. But of course we were dead tired, and slept like policemen; so when we awoke in the morning and ran to the window it was already too late, because it was half past eleven. It was a sharp disappointment. However, we ordered breakfast and told the landlady to call the Englishman, but she said he was already up and off at daybreak,—and swearing mad about something or other. We could not find out what the matter was. He had asked the landlady the altitude of her place above the level of the lake, and she had told him fourteen hundred and ninety-five feet. That was all that was said; then he lost his temper. He said that between fools and guide-books, a man could acquire ignorance enough in twenty-four hours in a country like this to last him a year. Harris believed our boy had been loading him up with misinformation; and this was probably the case, for his epithet described that boy to a dot.

We got under way about the turn of noon, and pulled out for the summit again, with a fresh and vigorous step. When we had gone about two hundred yards, and stopped to rest, I glanced to the left while I was lighting my pipe, and in the distance detected a long worm of black smoke crawling lazily up the steep mountain. Of course that was the locomotive. We propped ourselves on our elbows at once, to gaze, for we had never seen a mountain railway yet. Presently we could make out the train. It seemed incredible that that thing should creep straight up a sharp slant like the roof of a house,—but there it was, and it was doing that very miracle.

In the course of a couple of hours we reached a fine breezy altitude where the little shepherd-huts had big stones all over their roofs to hold them down to the earth when the great storms rage. The country was wild and rocky about here, but there were plenty of trees, plenty of moss, and grass.

Away off on the opposite shore of the lake we could see some villages, and now for the first time we could observe the real difference between their proportions and those of the giant mountains at whose feet they slept. When one is in one of those villages it seems spacious, and its houses seem high and not out of proportion to the mountain that overhangs them—but from our altitude, what a change! The mountains were bigger and grander than ever, as they stood there thinking their solemn thoughts with their heads in the drifting clouds, but the villages at their feet,—when the painstaking eye could trace them up and find them,—were so reduced, so almost invisible, and lay so flat against the ground, that the exactest simile I can devise is to compare them to ant-deposits of granulated dirt over-shadowed by the huge bulk of a cathedral. The steamboats skimming along under the stupendous precipices were diminished by distance to the daintiest little toys, the sail-boats and row-boats to shallops proper for fairies that keep house in the cups of lilies and ride to court on the backs of bumble-bees.

Presently we came upon half a dozen sheep nibbling grass in the spray of a

Mountain guide Paul Elter shows details of various ice techniques
and the ice of wildly rugged Bondasca glacier in the Bern highlands.

1. Ascent on a steep, icy slope without cutting steps. The front teeth of the crampons dig into the ice. Such climbing requires strong calf muscles. For safety reasons an ice screw has been applied.

2. Hacking uniform steps into the ice with an ice axe requires strength and skill. The steps have to be made in such a way that they can be used for the descent.

3. An ice screw will hold only if it is driven into solid ice. With a few strikes of his pick, the guide removes the top ice layer, which is usually somewhat brittle, before he drives the screw into the ice. Such a screw is used especially to provide a better foothold.

4. A strong sense of balance is needed to walk on the narrow ridge of a glacier. Here, too, the crampons give the mountaineer the necessary security.

5. Advancing technique on steep ice or perennial snow (firm). The mountaineer stands and walks on the front teeth of his crampons while keeping his upper body in balance with the help of his ice axe or a hook.

6. Straddling on ice. With the pick of the ice hammer, the right hand hacks out grips and, if necessary, steps, in the ice.

stream of clear water that sprang from a rock wall a hundred feet high, and all at once our ears were startled with a melodious "Lul . . . l . . . . l . . . . lul-lul-*lahee*-o-o-o!" pealing joyously from a near but invisible source, and recognized that we were hearing for the first time the famous Alpine *jodel* in its own native wilds. And we recognized, also, that it was that sort of quaint commingling of baritone and falsetto which at home we call "Tyrolese warbling."

The jodling (pronounced y*o*dling,—emphasis on the o,) continued, and was very pleasant and inspiriting to hear. Now the jodler appeared,—a shepherd boy of sixteen,—and in our gladness and gratitude we gave him a franc to jodel some more. So he jodeled, and we listened. We moved on, presently, and he generously jodeled us out of sight. After about fifteen minutes we came across another shepherd boy who was jodling, and gave him half a franc to keep it up. He also jodled us out of sight. After that, we found a jodler every ten minutes; we gave the first one eight cents, the second one six cents, the third one four, the fourth one a penny, contributed nothing to Nos. 5, 6, and 7, and during the remainder of the day hired the rest of the jodlers, at a franc apiece, not to jodel any more. There is somewhat too much of this jodling in the Alps.

About the middle of the afternoon we passed through a prodigious natural gateway called the Felsenthor, formed by two enormous upright rocks, with a third lying across the top. There was a very attractive little hotel close by, but our energies were not conquered yet, so we went on.

Three hours afterward we came to the railway track. It was planted straight up the mountain with the slant of a ladder that leans against a house, and it seemed to us that a man would need good nerves who proposed to travel up it or down it either.

During the latter part of the afternoon we cooled our roasting interiors with ice-cold water from clear streams, the only really satisfying water we had tasted since we left home, for at the hotels on the continent they merely give you a tumbler of ice to soak your water in, and that only modifies its hotness, doesn't make it cold. Water can only be made cold enough for summer comfort by being prepared in a refrigerator or a closed ice-pitcher. Europeans say ice water impairs digestion. How do they know?—they never drink any.

At ten minutes past six we reached the Kaltbad station, where there is a spacious hotel with great verandahs which command a majestic expanse of lake and mountain scenery. We were pretty well fagged out, now, but as we did not wish to miss the Alpine sunrise, we got through with our dinner as quickly as possible and hurried off to bed. It was unspeakably comfortable to stretch our weary limbs between the cool damp sheets. And how we did sleep!—for there is no opiate like Alpine pedestrianism.

In the morning we both awoke and leaped out of bed at the same instant and ran and stripped aside the window curtains; but we suffered a bitter disappointment again: it was already half past three in the afternoon.

We dressed sullenly and in ill spirits, each accusing the other of oversleeping. Harris said if we had brought the courier along, as we ought to have done, we should not have missed these sunrises. I said he knew very well that one of us would have to sit up and wake the courier; and I added that we were having trouble enough to take care of ourselves, on this climb, without having to take care of a courier besides.

During breakfast our spirits came up a little, since we found by the guide-book that in the hotels on the summit the tourist is not left to trust to luck for his sunrise, but is roused betimes by a man who goes through the halls with a great Alpine horn, blowing blasts that would raise the dead. And there was another consoling thing: the guide-book said that up there on the summit the guests did not wait to dress much, but seized a red bed-blanket and sailed out arrayed like an Indian. This was good; this would be romantic; two hundred and fity people grouped on the windy summit, with their hair flying and their red blankets flapping, in the solemn presence of the snowy ranges and the messenger splendors of the coming sun, would be a striking and memorable spectacle. So it was good luck, not ill luck, that we had missed those other sunrises.

We were informed by the guide-book that we were now 3,228 feet above the level of the lake,—therefore full two-thirds of our journey had been accomplished. We got away at a quarter past four, p.m.; a hundred yards above the hotel the railway divided; one track went straight up the steep hill, the other one turned square off to the right, with a very slight grade. We took the latter, and followed it more than a mile, turned a rocky corner and came in sight of a handsome new hotel. If we had gone on, we should have arrived at the summit, but Harris preferred to ask a lot of questions,—as usual, of a man who didn't know anything,—and he told us to go back and follow the other route. We did so. We could ill afford this loss of time.

We climbed, and climbed; and we kept on climbing; we reached about forty summits but there was always another one just ahead. It came on to rain, and it rained in dead earnest. We were soaked through, and it was bitter cold. Next a smoky fog of clouds covered the whole region densely, and we took to the railway ties to keep from getting lost. Sometimes we slopped along in a narrow path on the left hand side of the track, but by and by when the fog blew aside a little and we saw that we were treading the rampart of a precipice and that our left elbows were projecting over a perfectly boundless and bottomless vacancy, we gasped, and jumped for the ties again.

The night shut down, dark and drizzly and cold. About eight in the evening the fog lifted and showed us a well worn path which led up a very steep rise to the left. We took it and as soon as we had got far enough from the railway to render the finding it again an impossibility, the fog shut down on us once more.

We were in a bleak unsheltered place, now, and had to trudge right along, in order to keep warm, though we rather expected to go over a precipice sooner or

Roping down the Bondasca glacier. The double rope can be anchored to a "pair" hacked from the ice, a wooden peg driven in or a sacrificed ice pick.

later. About nine o'clock we made an important discovery—that we were not in any path. We groped around a while on our hands and knees, but could not find it; so we sat down in the mud and the wet scant grass to wait. We were terrified into this by being suddenly confronted with a vast body which showed itself vaguely for an instant and in the next instant was smothered in the fog again. It was really the hotel we were after, monstrously magnified by the fog, but we took it for the face of a precipice and decided not to try to claw up it.

We sat there an hour, with chattering teeth and quivering bodies, and quarreled over all sorts of trifles, but gave most of our attention to abusing each other for the stupidity of deserting the railway track. We sat with our backs to that precipice, because what little wind there was came from that quarter. At some time or other the fog thinned a little; we did not know when, for we were facing the empty universe and the thinness could not show; but at last Harris happened to look around, and there stood a huge, dim, spectral hotel where the precipice had been. One could faintly discern the windows and chimneys, and a dull blur of lights. Our first emotion was deep, unutterable gratitude, our next was a foolish rage, born of the suspicion that possibly the hotel had been visible three-quarters of an hour while we sat there in those cold puddles quarreling.

Yes, it was the Rigi-Kulm hotel—the one that occupies the extreme summit, and whose remote little sparkle of lights we had often seen glinting high aloft among the stars from our balcony away down yonder in Lucerne. The crusty portier and the crusty clerks gave us the surly reception which their kind deal in prosperous times, but by mollifying them with an extra display of obsequiousness and servility we finally got them to show us to the room which our boy had engaged for us.

We got into some dry clothing, and while our supper was preparing we loafed forsakenly through a couple of vast cavernous drawing rooms, one of which had a stove in it. This stove was in a corner, and densely walled around with people. We could not get near the fire, so we moved at large in the arctic spaces, among a multitude of people who sat silent, smileless, forlorn and shivering—thinking what fools they were to come, perhaps. There were some Americans, and some Germans, but one could see that the great majority were English.

We lounged into an apartment where there was a great crowd, to see what was going on. It was a memento-magazine. The tourists were eagerly buying all sorts and styles of paper-cutters, marked "Souvenir of the Rigi," with handles made of the little curved horn of the ostensible chamois; there were all manner of wooden goblets and such things, similarly marked. I was going to buy a paper-cutter, but I believed I could remember the cold comfort of the Rigi-Kulm without it, so I smothered the impulse.

Supper warmed us, and we went immediately to bed,—but first, as Mr. Baedeker requests all tourists to call his attention to any errors which they may

find in his guide-books, I dropped him a line to inform him that when he said the foot-journey from Wäggis to the summit was only three hours and a quarter, he missed it by just about three days. I had previously informed him of his mistake about the distance from Allerheiligen to Oppenau, and had also informed the Ordnance Department of the German government of the same error in the imperial maps. I will add, here, that I never got any answer to these letters, or any thanks from either of those sources; and what is still more discourteous, these corrections have not been made, either in the maps or the guide-books. But I will write again when I get time, for my letters may have miscarried.

We curled up in the clammy beds, and went to sleep without rocking. We were so sodden with fatigue that we never stirred nor turned over till the booming blasts of the Alpine horn aroused us. It may well be imagined that we did not lose any time. We snatched on a few odds and ends of clothing, cocooned ourselves in the proper red blankets, and plunged along the halls and out into the whistling wind bareheaded. We saw a tall wooden scaffolding on the very peak of the summit, a hundred yards away, and made for it. We rushed up the stairs to the top of this scaffolding, and stood there, above the vast outlying world, with hair flying and ruddy blankets waving and cracking in the fierce breeze.

"Fifteen minutes too late, at last!" said Harris, in a vexed voice. "The sun is clear above the horizon."

"No matter," I said, "it is a most magnificent spectacle, and we will see it do the rest of its rising, anyway."

In a moment we were deeply absorbed in the marvel before us, and dead to everything else. The great cloud-barred disk of the sun stood just above a limitless expanse of tossing white-caps,—so to speak,—a billowy chaos of massy mountain domes and peaks draped in imperishable snow, and flooded with an

Climbing the Fründerhorns (3,368 meters), on the lake, is easy under normal circumstances. After a change of weather the rocks are covered with ice and freshly fallen snow. On the steep, snowy slope, which leads to the peak, the members of a mountain-guide course follow the tracks in the deep fresh snow.

133

The Aletsch glacier is twenty-six kilometers long and the mightiest ice river of the Alps at Konkordia Square, where the Jungfrau firns, the big Aletsch firns, and the perennial snow field meet. Glacier experts have measured the thickness of the ice to be 600 to 800 meters. In the background the big Aletsch and the small Aletsch.

opaline glory of changing and dissolving splendors, whilst through rifts in a black cloud-bank above the sun, radiating lances of diamond dust shot to the zenith. The cloven valleys of the lower world swam in a tinted mist which veiled the ruggedness of their crags and ribs and ragged forests, and turned all the forbidding region into a soft and rich and sensuous paradise.

We could not speak. We could hardly breathe. We could only gaze in drunken ecstasy and drink it in. Presently Harris exclaimed,—

"Why——nation, it's going *down!*"

Perfectly true. We had missed the *morning* horn-blow, and slept all day. This was stupefying. Harris said,—

"Look here, the sun isn't the spectacle,—it's *us,*—stacked up here on top of this gallows, in these idiotic blankets, and two hundred and fifty well dressed men and women down here gawking up at us and not caring a straw whether the sun rises or sets, as long as they've got such a ridiculous spectacle as this to set down in their memorandum-books. They seem to be laughing their ribs loose, and there's one girl that there appears to be going all to pieces. I never saw such a man as you before. I think you are the very last possibility in the way of an ass."

"What have *I* done?" I answered with heat.

"What have you done?" You've got up at half past seven o'clock in the evening to see the sun rise, that's what you've done."

"And have you done any better, I'd like to know? I always used to get up with the lark, till I came under the petrifying influence of your turgid intellect."

"*You* used to get up with the lark,—O, no doubt,—you'll get up with the hangman one of these days. But you ought to be ashamed to be jawing here like this, in a red blanket, on a forty-foot scaffold on top of the Alps. And no end of people down here to boot; this isn't any place for an exhibition of temper."

And so the customary quarrel went on. When the sun was fairly down, we

134

slipped back to the hotel in the charitable gloaming, and went to bed again. We had encountered the horn-blower on the way, and he had tried to collect compensation, not only for announcing the sunset, which we did see, but for the sunrise, which we had totally missed; but we said no, we only took our solar rations on the "European plan"—pay for what you get. He promised to make us hear his horn in the morning, if we were alive.

He kept his word. We heard his horn and instantly got up. It was dark and cold and wretched. As I fumbled around for the matches, knocking things down with my quaking hands, I wished the sun would rise in the middle of the day, when it was warm and bright and cheerful, and one wasn't sleepy. We proceeded to dress by the gloom of a couple of sickly candles, but we could hardly button anything, our hands shook so. I thought of how many happy people there were in Europe, Asia and America, and everywhere, who were sleeping peacefully in their beds and did not have to get up and see the Rigi sunrise,—people who did

Short rest at the foot of Morgenhorns (3,612 meters), the easternmost peak of the Blümlis Alp group. Under favorable circumstances, traversing Morgenhorn–Weiss Frau–Blumlisalphorn is one of the most beautiful tours of the Bern highlands, but now the visibility is poor and the snow is much too soft. Nevertheless, mountain-guide candidates are on their way. They have to get to know the mountains under adverse conditions, too.

135

not appreciate their advantage, as like as not, but would get up in the morning wanting more boons of Providence. While thinking these thoughts I yawned, in a rather ample way, and my upper teeth got hitched on a nail over the door, and whilst I was mounting a chair to free myself, Harris drew the window curtain and said,—

"O, this is luck! We shan't have to go out at all,—yonder are the mountains, in full view."

That was glad news, indeed. It made us cheerful right away. One could see the grand Alpine masses dimly outlined against the black firmament, and one or two faint stars blinking through rifts in the night. Fully clothed, and wrapped in blankets, we huddled ourselves up, by the window, with lighted pipes, and fell into chat, while we waited in exceeding comfort to see how an Alpine sunrise was going to look by candle light. By and by a delicate, spiritual sort of effulgence spread itself by imperceptible degrees over the loftiest altitudes of the snowy wastes,—but there the effort seemed to stop. I said, presently,—

"There is a hitch about this sunrise somewhere. It doesn't seem to go. What do you reckon is the matter with it?"

"I don't know. It appears to hang fire somewhere. I never saw a sunrise act like that before. Can it be that the hotel is playing anything on us?"

"Of course not. The hotel merely has a property interest in the sun, it has nothing to do with the management of it. It is a precarious kind of property, too; a succession of total eclipses would probably ruin this tavern. Now what can be the matter with this sunrise?"

Harris jumped up and said,—

"I've got it! I know what's the matter with it! We've been looking at the place where the sun *set* last night!"

"It is perfectly true! Why couldn't you have thought of that sooner? Now we've lost another one! And all through your blundering. It was exactly like you to light a pipe and sit down to wait for the sun to rise in the west."

"It was exactly like me to find out the mistake, too. You never would have found it out. I find out all the mistakes."

"You make them all, too, else your most valuable faculty would be wasted on you. But don't stop to quarrel, now,—maybe we are not too late yet."

But we were. The sun was well up when we got to the exhibition ground.

On our way up we met the crowd returning—men and women dressed in all sorts of queer costumes, and exhibiting all degrees of cold and wretchedness in their gaits and countenances. A dozen still remained on the ground when we reached there, huddled together about the scaffold with their backs to the bitter wind. They had their red guide-books open at the diagram of the view, and were painfully picking out the several mountains and trying to impress their names and positions on their memories. It was one of the saddest sights I ever saw.

136

Two sides of this place were guarded by railings, to keep people from being blown over the precipices. The view, looking sheer down into the broad valley, eastward, from this great elevation,—almost a perpendicular mile,—was very quaint and curious. Counties, towns, hilly ribs and ridges, wide stretches of green meadow, great forest tracts, winding streams, a dozen blue lakes, a flock of busy steamboats—we saw all this little world in unique circumstantiality of detail —saw it just as the birds see it—and all reduced to the smallest of scales and as sharply worked out and finished as a steel engraving. The numerous toy villages, with tiny spires projecting out of them, were just as the children might have left them when done with play the day before; the forest tracts were diminished to cushions of moss; one or two big lakes were dwarfed to ponds, the smaller ones to puddles,—though they did not look like puddles, but like blue ear-drops which had fallen and lodged in slight depressions, conformable to their shapes, among the moss-bed and the smooth levels of dainty green farm-land; the microscopic steamboats glided along, as in a city reservoir, taking a mighty time to cover the distance between ports which seemed only a yard apart and the isthmus which separated two lakes looked as if one might stretch out on it and lie with both elbows in the water, yet we knew invisible wagons were toiling across it and finding the distance a tedious one. This beautiful miniature world had exactly the appearance of those "relief maps" which reproduce nature precisely, with the heights and depressions and other details graduated to a reduced scale, and with the rocks, trees, lakes, etc., colored after nature.

I believed we could walk down to Wäggis or Vitznau in a day, but I knew we could go down by rail in about an hour, so I chose the latter method. I wanted to see what it was like, anyway. The train came along about the middle of the forenoon, and an odd thing it was. The locomotive boiler stood on end, and it and the whole locomotive were tilted sharply backward. There were two passen-

The Bern Alps as seen from the Bishorn in Wallis. Who can count the peaks and know their names? New views open forever to the mountaineer. New goals beckon him forever. Not so much the goal, but the adventure to conquer the mountain, brings fulfillment.

137

ger cars, roofed, but wide open all around. These cars were not tilted back, but the seats were; this enables the passenger to sit level while going down a steep incline.

There are three railway tracks; the central one is cogged; the "lantern wheel" of the engine grips its way along these cogs, and pulls the train up the hill or retards its motion on the down trip. About the same speed,—three miles an hour,—is maintained both ways. Whether going up or down, the locomotive is always at the lower end of the train. It pushes, in the one case, braces back in the other. The passenger rides backward, going up, and faces forward going down.

We got front seats, and while the train moved along about fifty yards on level ground, I was not the least frightened; but now it started abruptly down stairs, and I caught my breath. And I, like my neighbors, unconsciously held back all I could, and threw my weight to the rear, but of course that did no particular good. I had slidden down the balusters when I was a boy, and thought nothing of it, but to slide down the balusters in a railway train is a thing to make one's flesh creep. Sometimes we had as much as ten yards of almost level ground, and this gave us a few full breaths in comfort; but straightway we would turn a corner and see a long steep line of rails stretching down below us, and the comfort was at an end. One expected to see the locomotive pause, or slack up a little, and approach this plunge cautiously, but it did nothing of the kind; it went calmly on, and when it reached the jumping-off place it made a sudden bow, and went gliding smoothly down stairs, untroubled by the circumstances. . . .

There was no level ground at the Kaltbad station; the railbed was as steep as a roof; I was curious to see how the stop was going to be managed. But it was very simple: the train came sliding down, and when it reached the right spot it just stopped—that was all there was "to it"—stopped on the steep incline, and when the exchange of passengers and baggage had been made, it moved off and went sliding down again. The train can be stopped anywhere, at a moment's notice. . . .

By the time one reaches Kaltbad, he has acquired confidence in the railway, and he now ceases to try to ease the locomotive by holding back. Thenceforward he smokes his pipe in serenity, and gazes out upon the magnificent picture below and about him with unfettered enjoyment. There is nothing to interrupt the view or the breeze; it is like inspecting the world on the wing. However,—to be exact,—there is one place where the serenity lapses for a while: this is while one is crossing the Schnurrtobel Bridge, a frail structure which swings its gossamer frame down through the dizzy air, over a gorge, like a vagrant spider-strand.

One has no difficulty in remembering his sins while the train is creeping down this bridge; and he repents of them, too; though he sees, when he gets to Vitznau, that he need not have done it, the bridge was perfectly safe.

So ends the eventful trip which we made to the Rigi-Kulm to see an Alpine sunrise.